THE SAVVY SPENDER

How to make, save
and grow your wealth
in seven simple steps

MEGAN
MICKLEWRIGHT

HARRIMAN HOUSE
www.harriman-house.com

First published in 2026 by Harriman House, an imprint of Pan Macmillan
EU Representative: Macmillan Publishers Ireland Ltd, 1st Floor, The Liffey Trust Centre, 117-126 Sheriff Street Upper, Dublin 1, D01 YC43
Associated companies throughout the world
www.panmacmillan.com

Paperback ISBN: 978-1-80409-312-2
eBook ISBN: 978-1-80409-313-9
Audio ISBN: 978-1-80409-314-6

British Library Cataloguing in Publication Data
A CIP catalogue record for this book can be obtained from the British Library.

01

Printed and bound by CPI Group (UK) Ltd.
Cover Design by Charlotte Smith, Adobe Stock Images used.

THE SAVVY SPENDER

CONTENTS

PREFACE: ME, MYSELF AND I

I'M SO GLAD you're here and decided to pick up this book. I think it's fair for me to make the assumption that you're somewhat interested in what this book has to offer – you're looking for a guide to help you make, save and grow your money. Well, you're in the right place, and have I got some brilliant chapters for you to get stuck into! We'll be diving into how money really works in the real world, how to spend intentionally, how to build a savings pot that'll actually stick around, and how to secure a more financially savvy future… (and of course so much more).

Whether you're feeling too busy, overwhelmed with your finances or like you've tried everything before – this book differs from others you might have tried because it's been written to help you create habits, mindset changes and systems that fit your life, your goals, and your values.

So, you're reading my book, but you might be wondering: Who am I?

I am Megan Micklewright, though you may know me as *The Savvy Spender*.

I'm a money expert, award-winning financial influencer, investor, presenter, commercial model, mother, and oh, I nearly forgot… an author! (It's going to take some time to get used to that last one!)

It's not always been this way, though. I didn't become any of those things overnight. Like anyone who wants to grow their financial literacy and wealth, I had to undergo a process of change, during which I made and learned from many mistakes. I had to discover the deeper meaning of money and, most importantly, the mindset that you must adopt to take control of your finances and your future.

Where did it all start?

I grew up on a council estate in Birmingham, with parents who worked hard to make ends meet. They split up when I was young, and my dad left my mum in a load of debt from setting up a business (a failed one!) that caused her to declare bankruptcy. This was when I first became aware of the money issues within our household and realised how important money is. I never liked asking for money, because I knew there wasn't much of it, so at a young age I took money-making matters into my own hands.

It helped that I had always seen my mum try to make extra money in creative ways. I remember her posting handmade leaflets advertising her cleaning services through the doors of other houses on the estate. She gained a few regular clients that way, and she'd clean their homes around her other work commitments. I also remember her coming home with black bags full of ironing, and I'd watch TV in the living room of an evening while she'd make her way through the content of the bags, all in the name of keeping the household afloat. Subconsciously, this must have sparked the fire of entrepreneurship in me, and given me that drive to try creative ways to make some cash.

The start of entrepreneurship

I attended secondary school at Grace Academy in Chelmsley Wood. During my time there, I experienced entrepreneurship in action without even realising it – because money was always on my mind!

I used to spend my lunch money to buy snacks (chocolates, drinks and crisps) from Poundland in Chelmsley Wood Town Centre and sell them to other children from my flowery Cath Kidston backpack. I was the only girl who did this, so I had a captive market and usually made a little profit. I'd use my earnings to fund trips out with my friends at the weekends, instead of having to ask my mum for money. I must admit, I didn't earn much from this small side quest, so I was always racking my brain for new ideas and ways to make money. This led to other money makers – and while still in school, I ran a string of different side hustles ('earners' is what we used to call them), including:

- Personalised bracelets
- Personalised masks
- Avon (in my mum's name!)

This really gave me the taste for earning my own money. At such a young age, having my own little stash was empowering. It was my first little taste of growing and managing my own money.

Once I left school, it was my goal to earn as much money as I possibly could, which led to me working three part-time jobs at once (in a mix of stores: Sports Direct, New Look and Brantano (bonus points if you remember that one!) while also studying A-levels at college. I took any shifts I could, working late after college, early mornings on weekends and any other time I could fit in – all to earn as much money as possible.

I actually dropped out of college because at the time I felt like earning money was more important than my education. I wanted to earn rather than learn, which just proves how desperate I was for money.

Now I know that education is the most important thing you need if you want to earn more money.

The more you learn, the more you earn!

Having three part-time jobs wasn't very sustainable, and I quickly realised I needed something more concrete. After a chat with my mum, I decided to go down the apprenticeship route. I ended up on a human resources apprenticeship at a very well-known football club. Learning while earning was the best thing for someone like me. Money was still a priority, but I knew I needed qualifications too. Getting both was definitely the best of both worlds. This was the first stepping stone of my corporate career (which I maintained alongside a string of side hustles, of course!).

I climbed the corporate ladder, moving between companies and landing small pay rises along the way (with a random stint in Farmfoods' head office somewhere in between). Meanwhile, the side hustles I continued to run included selling flower boxes on Instagram, spending my weekends driving to and from baby showers to set up decorations, and running a vegan bakery in our local community centre (the last would become another victim of the Covid-19 pandemic lockdowns).

Although I was in great jobs and a great position for my age, I knew there had to be something more. My spark for entrepreneurship was always lit. I could never quite put my finger on *how* I knew, but I was sure that working in a corporate environment on a fixed salary wasn't for me. I just didn't know how to change the situation at the time. This changed during the pandemic lockdowns. Most of the people I knew were off work on furlough, while I was still working. Yes, I was very annoyed (i.e., jealous). It made me realise time is precious, it's not all about the money, it's about freedom and choices, living your life on your own time and terms.

Throughout the years I got savvier with the way I handled money, learning crucial life lessons such as 'novelty wears off' (living by this motto has saved me thousands, and I highly recommend you try it too if you always want to have money in your pocket). But it wasn't until a little later that I started to see these habits as part of a much larger framework of financial understanding.

That shift happened when my partner introduced me to the author Robert Kiyosaki and his book *Rich Dad Poor Dad*. This book really confirmed that the way I felt about my finances wasn't unusual; it was actually very common. However, it *was* rare in the area that I grew up in.

I knew the way I was handling money in the physical sense was right, but I realised I still had a lot to learn about the world and mindset of finance. The trouble was that every lesson went against the grain of the family and community that I grew up in. I was learning a completely new way of navigating money. This is where my partner played a huge part in my money mindset journey. Ironically, he grew up on a council estate just like me (but in a worse area), his mum worked a lot, so he had lots of free time, alone as a kid. We always say this made him into the 'free spirit' that he is, and this free spirit is what led him to read finance books from a very young age. He knew what most people learn about money in their 30s, in his mid-teens. He was the one who switched on the light bulb in my brain to financial topics such as:

- Investing
- The importance of liquid cash
- Good debt versus bad debt

- Going against societal money norms
- The emotional side of money

By the time I'd learned a good chunk of what I now know, I didn't want to keep it all to myself. So, while pregnant with my first child, I founded The Savvy Spender.

While I was on maternity leave from my then full-time job at a huge tech company, I realised that maternity pay was not a lot to survive on. Just like in my childhood, I didn't want to have to rely on anybody else for money, so I went back to my entrepreneurial ways and started doing side hustles to top up my pay, things like: market researches, site surveys, website testing, mystery shopping, receipt scanning and bank switches. I was soon making around an extra £500–£1,000 a month on top of my maternity pay (and yes, if you're on statutory maternity pay (SMP), this is allowed).

I realised how hard other women must find the drop in pay! SMP really is pennies to live on. So I began sharing my savvy ways, side hustle tips and tricks. Before I knew it, this was helping women across the country to save and make extra money.

Growing The Savvy Spender has been a huge adventure that I won't detail exhaustively, but here's a highlight reel of some of my most recent 'wow' moments:

- Independently helping thousands of people get through one of the worst economic crises in history.
- Working with some of the biggest financial brands in the world, including the likes of BlackRock.
- Meeting with former prime minister, Rishi Sunak.
- Receiving invitations to Downing Street.
- Being crowned Online Financial Influencer of the Year.
- Becoming a financial presenter.

- Winning multiple awards as a financial influencer.[1]

The Savvy Spender is where I share everything I've learned about money, from those early lessons in my childhood to the latest ones I've picked up from my ongoing self-education. After all, as Jim Rohn said, "Formal education will make you a living; self-education will make you a fortune." One reason this is true is that formal education has a 'finish line' in the form of a degree or other qualification, whereas self-education never ends.

Because trust me, there's always something more to learn when it comes to money.

Don't get me wrong, formal education has its place – and let me tell you I have spent tens of thousands of pounds gaining formal education, but self-education is a timeless and limitless realm!

Over the years I have learned so much about enjoying your life whilst still getting the most from your money. It's such a common misconception that to save and be good with money you must not enjoy it, but I'm here to tell you, that's a load of sh**. As long as your good money habits outweigh your bad money habits, you're on the road to financial stability! Don't you worry, we're going to get into alllllll of that.

I am going to dive into how to make, save and grow your money whether you earn six or seven figures or have mothballs in your bank account. Wherever you're starting from, the seven simple steps I cover here will help you to improve your relationship with money as well as the contents of your account. I know this because these are the same steps my partner and I have taken to create real financial stability for our family. We no longer trade our time for money, and instead we raise our kids with both parents at home, while also building generational wealth.

So what happened?

I bet you're thinking what the hell happened in-between the girl who sold chocolates out of her backpack at school to cementing my role as a trusted voice in the industry.

Well it's a good job we've got a lot of time together in this book to help you find out!

Once you have finished reading this book, you will essentially have my head on your shoulders. The way I think and feel about money will become your way of thinking and feeling about money. You will be your very own Savvy Spender, your very own personal award-winning money expert!

How good does that sound?

I wish I had that… oh wait…

INTRODUCTION: WHAT IS MONEY MINDSET?

'MONEY MINDSET' is more than just a buzzword you hear in finance books or on social media. It's the belief system that you hold about money, and it starts to form at a very young age.

It's the map of what you believe about what money actually *is*, how it makes you feel, how you perceive it to work, how people manage to make it, how hard (or easy) it is to get. And whether you realise it or not, your money mindset is at play *Every. Single. Day.*

Your money mindset impacts *everything*. How you spend, how you save, how you earn, how you feel about yourself, and even how you feel when others around you talk about money.

If you've ever:

- Avoided looking at your bank account because you'd prefer not to know what it's going to show you.
- Felt guilty for buying yourself something nice, even though you have the money to do so.
- Bought something you know you're not going to use just because you liked the look of it.

These are all elements of your money mindset in action!

If you struggle with any of these issues, or in any other part of your relationship with money, nothing will really change until you change your money mindset. No tips and tricks will stick. Not a budget, not a savings challenge, not even a pay rise.

This introductory chapter will help you understand the 'why' behind your money habits – why you think about money the way you do – and how we can change the things that need to be changed.

Once you do change your money mindset, believe me, managing money becomes easier. Your relationship with money becomes more positive, even enjoyable.

I enjoy everything about money. There's not a day that goes by that I don't talk about money – yet we live in a society where the entire topic is so taboo, so private. You might currently feel this way too, but we're going to change that narrative.

Spoiler alert: it's never just about the money

Money is never just that. It's so much more than its face value.

Money is:

- Safety
- Freedom
- Options
- Control

When I was younger, I saw money as the key to survival, and also something to feel awkward about, because nobody wanted to speak openly about it. Growing up on a council estate, money was tight, and it wasn't just our household living in that reality, it was the whole grove, the whole estate, even (except for those people in the bought houses, many of whom paid my mum to clean them!). My parents worked hard but didn't make enough to keep us out of money problems. Like most parents, they never *told* me about these problems, but you pick up on things as a kid, don't you?

When they split up, things got harder and my mum ended up declaring bankruptcy – twice. Did you know there's actually costs you have to pay to declare yourself bankrupt? Who'd have thought it!

One of my first memories of money that I ever so slightly remember, is my mum crying in the kitchen over a letter asking for money. I don't know what it was, or how much they were asking for, but I knew it must have been bad.

That was the moment I realised money was *more than just money*, it was stress, failure, sacrifice and struggle. When I read this back, that memory lives in my head again, my mum with her head in her hands, crying over that bill. 'Damn, was money really this bad?'

My money mindset was being mapped out even then. I came to believe that money was essentially *negative*, and that stuck with me for a while. No one taught me this intentionally, it was simply something I picked up at a young age.

We all go through the same process – although our experiences and the beliefs they inspire can be completely different, depending on our surroundings and circumstances.

These beliefs will stick with us unless something interrupts them. So much of society believes that 'money doesn't buy happiness' and that money 'is the root of all evil', and while this comes down to personal opinion, how many of us just believe these things because society told us they were true?

Here's another truth: money makes the world go around. As such it's something we have to manage, earn and use every day. So why not build a positive relationship with it? Why not learn to utilise it properly?

Over the years, I began to unpick the 'negative money' beliefs that I'd picked up on throughout my childhood, and I started to form my own opinions about money, things that I didn't just pick up accidentally and learn out of habit from the struggles that I'd seen years ago. Through learning, listening, experiences and a lot of self-education, I started to see money as something different.

Fast-forward to now: money to me means freedom and options. Money is in abundance, and I am in control of how much I earn, how much I need for the things I need and want in my life. I've changed *what money means* to me, and here's how you can learn to change what money means to *you*.

What does money mean to you?

Have you ever actually asked yourself what money means to you, or even been asked that question by somebody else? I want you to take a moment to think about your answer.

In today's society money is a taboo subject. It's something we need to keep private and not speak about with others. We're seen as shallow if we care about money too much – but really, why shouldn't we? We need money to live, and I for one think a lot of people don't care about money enough. I want you to sit on that thought, and really think about what it means to you, not *what you've been told it should mean* to you, not what society thinks, but what *you* think about money and its place in your life.

A pinnacle moment for me

There'll be moments in your life that'll really cement a feeling about money into your beliefs and mindset. You'll have already had some throughout your life that have gotten you to where you are now.

It's important to differentiate between the moments that are pushing you forward, and the ones that are holding you back.

Let me tell you about a pinnacle moment for me, something that pushed me forward and really made me think differently about money in a way I didn't even know was possible.

I've spent thousands on my education, and let me tell you it can always feel like a risk. Online courses in particular might help you achieve financial freedom or just end up being expensive entertainment.

Well, I was on the most expensive training course I had ever paid for – and for this one money lesson alone, it was worth every penny. I watched someone make £15,000 in less than ten minutes. Ten minutes! They sold five £3,000 deals in front of my eyes. It was like something in my DNA changed there and then. I still can't even really put it into words how it made me feel.

I'd been programmed my whole life to think that making money was hard to do, that you have to work tirelessly, that there's not much to go around. Yet here, someone had made £15,000 more or less in the click of a finger. It was solid proof to me that money moves fast, and there's a lot of it, you just need to find out how to go and get it. That moment completely shifted how I saw money. I couldn't unsee it. I couldn't go back to just waiting for my time. I had to *do something*.

My whole life I had been taught self-limiting money beliefs, and now someone I barely knew had shown me the opposite – that anything is possible, and that money really is in abundance.

Where your money beliefs come from (and why they're holding you back)

So where do our money beliefs come from? Of course we're not born with limiting beliefs about money, we're taught them, and most of the time we don't even realise this is happening (and the people teaching us are usually doing it subconsciously).

Your money mindset is shaped by so many things. Some of these being:

- What you saw growing up.
- What gender you are and the gender roles in your society.
- What your parents said about money (does "money doesn't grow on trees!" ring a bell?).
- What your community, culture or religion told you ("Money doesn't buy happiness," for example).
- What you experienced during big life events such as job promotions, redundancies, getting your first credit card.
- What TV shows and social media have reinforced.

In the Preface, I mentioned that I was the only *girl* buying snacks from Poundland then selling them out of my flowery backpack at school. Why was that?

Because hustling and earning were not seen as 'girly'.

Looking back, I realise how early these gendered beliefs around money start.

On average, women still earn less than men across nearly every industry.

Let that sink in.

Women are less likely to invest than men, not because they're worse at it (in fact, research shows they often outperform men) but because they're less confident with money decisions.[2]

Women have been conditioned to believe that 'money stuff' is for men. That men should take care of the household finances. That rich people are all men. Just look at the finance bros. Male CEOs. Crypto lads on TikTok.

But here's what I've learned from experience, and from helping thousands of women with their finances: women *are* good with money. The problem is that, until recently, women haven't been given the tools, confidence or community to realise it.

Now, this book isn't just for women (so, dear reader, if you're of the male persuasion, don't slam it shut just yet). This book is for *anyone* who wants to understand and improve their relationship with money. Naturally though, as a woman who's had to work my way up from the ground, and seeing women struggle with their limiting money beliefs more than anybody else, helping women shift their mindset is something I'm massively passionate about.

This is just one example of how much other people (your parents, teachers, friends, the media) shape the way you think and feel about money. Most of our beliefs weren't chosen by us. They were absorbed, copied or handed down.

Now it's time to decide which ones you want to keep.

Because whether you're male, female, young, old, skint or currently sitting comfortably, if your mindset isn't right, your money won't be either!

Your first memory of money

Can you remember your first memory of money? I want you to think back to the earliest moment you remember feeling something emotional about money, whether that's a positive or not so positive emotion.

Maybe it was:

- Being told you couldn't have something because it was too expensive.
- Watching your parents argue about money or bills.
- Being given pocket money and spending it all on sweets.
- Saving up for something and feeling good about it.

Now, ask yourself:

- What emotion do you feel when you recall that memory?
- What belief could have been formed in that moment?
- Does that belief still exist now?

It's wild how much our financial behaviour as an adult is still based on what our seven-year-old self went through. I promise you though, it's never too late to change it.

How to break the cycle and reframe your thinking

So how can you break the cycle and start to reframe your thinking? Well, you're already on the first step right now: awareness! You're here, reading this book, so you're aware! Now it's time to re-write the narrative going on in your brain.

Let's take a few common limiting money beliefs, that I'm sure we've all heard, and flip each one on its head:

- "I'm not good with money" becomes "I'm learning how to be better with money."
- I just can't save" becomes "I'm building my savings step by step, and small amounts do count."
- "I need to earn more, but I can't" becomes "There are always new ways to grow my income."
- "Money is stressful" becomes "I'm creating a plan that gives me peace of mind with money."
- "Budgeting is restrictive" becomes "Budgeting helps me stay in control and enjoy life without the stress of overspending."

- "I'm bad at maths, so I can't manage money" becomes "I don't need to be a maths genius, I just need easy systems in place to manage my money."
- "People like me don't get rich" becomes "I'm breaking the cycle and creating a new money story for me and my family."

Reframing our mind takes time. We can't just undo everything we've learned over years and years, but now that you're aware, every time you catch yourself in a limiting belief you will know how to reframe it into a more empowering thought.

Steps to build a positive money mindset

Rome wasn't built in a day, nor will reframing your money mindset happen instantly. I still have old limiting beliefs crop up from time to time. It's only natural. Think of this as a journey, a never-ending one at that. There are always new tricks, new tips to learn along the way, but with a bit of commitment, you can create a healthier and happier relationship with money.

If you're wondering, *how do I do that?* I'm going to give you the step-by-step guide so you don't have to figure it out by yourself.

1. You need to be clear on your *why*

This sounds so cliché, but it's the most important step. Knowing *why* you're doing what you're doing gives you the motivation to keep going on the hard days, whether that's being consistent at the gym, quitting smoking, eating healthier, getting through your uni exams – your *why* is the reason you stick to these things!

So, why do you actually want to change your money mindset?

Perhaps your *why* isn't clear enough to articulate right now. If your mind has gone blank, here's a few common reasons why people want to change their money mindset:

- To get out of debt and stay out of debt.
- To stop living paycheck to paycheck.
- To build a better future for their family.
- To teach their kids better money habits.

These are just inspiration. Your reason doesn't have to be remotely similar to any of these, because it's personal to you. Once you know your why, make sure you write it down and keep it somewhere close. I like to write everything in my phone notes so it's easily accessible and I can refer back to things when I need that reminder.

It's important to revisit your why when things feel tough. When you feel old thoughts and limiting beliefs crop back up, it really will keep you focused.

2. Be hyper-aware of your money thoughts

A lot of the time, people don't realise they are having their own self-limiting thoughts about money, but tracking those thoughts as they come and go is important. You need to be hyper-aware of these, especially in the early days.

Have you ever thought, *I'm just not good with money*? I've heard this phrase a worrying number of times. It's a worrying belief because once someone says it, they just continue to believe it and don't try to *do* anything about it. The thing is, everyone can be good with money, but most people haven't even *tried* to be. I mean, why would we try? We haven't really ever been told the importance of being good with money, we're not taught financial literacy in school and my parents for sure didn't teach me anything about money (other than those subconscious lessons about money being stressful).

If you have ever thought, *I'm just not good with money*, there's a high chance that you'll think it again, and again, and again. You have to recognise this as a self-limiting belief. Recognise the thought, and then you can stop it in its tracks.

3. Start flipping the script

Each time you observe a self-limiting thought emerge, practice turning it on its head. Whether or not you believe it at the time, consistency becomes habit and eventually these self-limiting thoughts will turn into empowering thoughts. For every negative money thought you have, write it down and replace it with a positive one. It's not good enough to just do it in your head, you need to write it down, visualise it. There's a reason many people swear by journaling their thoughts. Getting it down on paper makes it physical, makes it more real. Most importantly, it makes it *stick*.

Instead of *I'm bad with money*, write *I'm learning to manage my money better every day*.

Instead of *money is stressful*, write *money is a tool I can use to create freedom*.

I'm not going to lie, this will probably feel a bit cringe at first, but believe me it'll start to feel a lot more natural the more you practice, and you'll eventually feel your mindset starting to shift.

I know it's easy to think of this kind of 'affirmation' approach as a tad 'woo woo' but there is real psychology behind it. Affirmations work by slowly reshaping the way we think, thanks to a process called *neuroplasticity* – the brain's ability to form new connections. When you repeat a phrase regularly, you're essentially training your brain to replace old, limiting money beliefs with empowering new ones.

Not only that, affirmations also create a moment of *pause* in order to reflect, which can interrupt those negative thoughts about money. Over time, this shift in mindset influences your behaviour.

People who practise affirmations are more likely to take action, whether that's starting a side hustle, sticking to a budget or finally setting up that savings account.

To be clear, affirmations aren't magic, and I don't believe in that 'think it into existence' mindset. They don't just make things work or change things simply because you've said them. But they can change your mindset and approach towards money, giving you the confidence and motivation to actually do the work that leads to that money mindset change and growth.

4. Get rid of the bad vibes

Your environment is everything. Just like how your mum didn't want you hanging around the wrong people in school because they were bad influences, I don't want you around people who will talk negatively about money and let those limiting beliefs creep back in.

Keep your money circle positive. Get rid of any triggers (these will be personal to you). Maybe you follow an influencer who lives a super lavish lifestyle that makes you think, *I could never live like that* – hit the unfollow button, or use that as motivation! On the flip side, follow more positive money influencers (like me).

5. Find your dopamine buzz in the small money wins

Spending money gives us a dopamine hit. That's why retail therapy exists – it makes us feel good, even if it was an impulse spend and hours later we regret blowing all of our monthly pay on something we'll probably never use.

What's great is that you can also start to feel this way about *saving* money. Celebrate those small wins and get that dopamine hit from them. Every time you make a more mindful money decision, stop an impulse buy, save towards your holiday or new house goal, you can get that same satisfaction. It may not be as instant, but the feeling will last a lot longer and be much more rewarding in the long run.

6. Keep learning

The journey never ends, and there's always something new to learn, which is a good thing! Money is always evolving, and the world around us is constantly changing – which means money is too. Never stop learning about money. As I mentioned earlier, "The more you learn, the more you earn."

7. Be kind to yourself

This might be the last step, but it's a very important one. One impulse spend doesn't ruin your progress. There will be times your old habits slip back in. That's okay, as long as you don't let them win! If one of the tyres on your car got punctured, would you go and put holes in the other three? Of course not! So don't undo all of your progress and hard work if you have a few slip-ups, they're normal and it's all part of the process. Remember, your money mindset was built over years, it's going to take time to re-write.

Let's rewind and recap:

Money isn't just money. It's emotions. It's freedom. It's options.

It's habits!

You *can* reframe that money mindset.

Make those wins visible. Track them, celebrate them. Stop those self-limiting beliefs in their tracks and replace them with empowering ones. Keep your circle positive, and most importantly remember your *why*.

Money mindset really is everything. I know people earning six figures who still *feel* broke, and that's because their mindset is still self-limiting. They haven't equipped themselves with the tools to manage money in the right way. You can't keep a bucket riddled with holes full of water, can you? In the same way, you can't manage money if you don't equip yourself with the tools you need.

Being rich isn't actually about the amount of money you earn, it's about your money mindset and how you manage the money you do have. Change your thoughts. Celebrate the small wins. Build the life you want.

Scarcity versus abundance

I want to address two of the most common mindsets around money. Though there are many nuances to each, the chances are good that your overall money mindset falls into one of these categories. Think of them as pre-loaded collections of money thoughts and feelings. They are the *scarcity mindset* and the *abundance mindset.*

Scarcity (oops, this was me!)

A scarcity mindset is all about fear. It's a voice in your head that says, *what if I lose it all?* or *there's not enough money to go around.* When you live with a scarcity mindset, you tend to grip onto money as tightly as possible. You save for the sake of saving, you hesitate to spend on yourself, and you often miss out on opportunities because you'd prefer to save than spend in fear that you may run out of money.

I've lived in this mindset before. It definitely came from seeing the money struggles in my household at a young age, and that mindset doesn't just change. Scarcity thoughts crop up all the time.

For me, it meant that I would hoard money, even when spending it might have improved my life or actually saved me money in the long run. Holding onto every penny sounds sensible, and of course saving is important, but there's a point where it actually stops being healthy. Ironically, the more you cling to money out of fear, the more restricted you feel.

Abundance

This doesn't mean you're reckless or pretending money grows on trees. It means you view money as something that flows. It comes in, it goes out, and it can always be created again.

People with an abundance mindset invest in themselves, say yes to opportunities, and use their money in ways that add value to their lives. They believe there's always another way to earn more, and this belief itself often opens the doors to new opportunities. This is my partner all over, and having opposite mind frames really has helped me to come such a long way with my money mindset.

We all dip in and out of both mindsets. Some days you might feel abundant, other days scarcity steps in. It's all about noticing when scarcity is driving your money decisions and being able to identify whether those decisions are sensible and rational or being driven by the voice inside your head that is scared to spend.

When you move closer to an abundance mindset, money stops being a source of anxiety and starts being what it was always meant to be, which is a tool to help you create the life you want.

Work that confidence

Confidence shapes who we are. It defines how we carry ourselves, what risks we take, what opportunities we come across and even how we manage and control our money.

When we believe we can learn, grow and handle finances well, it shows in our confidence. But if deep down you believe you're just not good with money, that belief holds you back (believe me, I hear this all the time). It stops you from asking for what you deserve.

Almost half of UK adults don't feel confident managing their day-to-day money.[3] Nearly half of people aren't talking to anyone about their finances, even though many wish they could.[4] Silence keeps confidence low!

Mistakes will be made, which isn't failure, it's a lesson learned. These lessons teach you to be more confident with money, they teach you what works and what doesn't. None of us start perfect. If it helps, you should know that I'm still not perfect now. In fact, I don't think you *can* ever be perfect with money. The journey of financial confidence isn't about never failing, it's about learning, adapting, and moving forward.

Your goals are what this is all for. Confidence helps you move towards those goals. When you know your *why*, when you can welcome mistakes and learn from them, that's when you can really make positive steps towards your goals.

Work to live, or live to work?

This is one of those questions that gives old-school motivational speech vibes, but it's actually a question that can really influence your money and your mindset. Most of us were raised on the idea that hard work is everything, even as early as school days it's drilled into us... Listen and work hard, to get good grades, so you can get a 'good job' and climb that corporate ladder, work long hours, and one day you'll reap the rewards and enjoy life. Without being all doom and gloom, sometimes 'one day' never comes.

Living to work means your job controls you, your time and your energy. Sometimes your whole identity is tied up in what you do for a living. What's one of the first things you get asked when you meet someone new? "What do you do for a living?" or just "What do you do?" People don't even bother to add "for a living" half the time. The assumption is that our work defines who we are, and it often does define how people view us.

But our jobs shouldn't define us. Because – let's address the elephant in the room here – if we didn't need the money, few of us would still be doing the job we're doing just out of the goodness of our hearts. But as things are, the average person spends more than a third of their life at work![5]

Don't get me wrong, work can be fulfilling, and earning money is obviously essential, but this is the key difference. If you're spending all of your best years working non-stop, waiting for retirement before you live your life, you've got it the wrong way around.

Working to live, on the other hand, means knowing that the job you're doing is giving you money which can be used as a tool to help you towards the life you want to live. This doesn't mean you don't work hard; it means you're intentional about why you're working and where your money is going. You know your *why* and you make sure your career supports that life, rather than swallowing it up and giving you no time for anything else.

When you're mindful with your spending, saving, and earning, you stop chasing more for the sake of more.

The shift from living to work to working to live is one of the most freeing things you can do for yourself. Because earning money isn't just about surviving.

The generational shift

Our attitudes towards money are shaped by the generations before us. We inherit beliefs, habits and values.

For many of us, our grandparents grew up in a time when stability was everything. A steady job, a roof over your head, food on the table – that was success. Times were very different when they were young, and even when our parents were young. Some lived through wars, rationing or times of scarcity, so their mindset was built on survival and security. For them, working hard and being loyal to one employer was the complete norm and provided them with exactly what they needed.

This same mindset was passed down to our parents, but even then, times were shifting. That narrative of 'work hard, buy a house, stay in one job and get a good retirement' worked for some, but not as successfully as it had for the generation before. We started to see new challenges, like economic crashes, inflation and job market competition.

Now we're living in a completely different world. Lifetime jobs hardly exist anymore, not to mention that wages don't always keep up with the cost of living. Job hopping has become a very sensible thing to do to increase your income, which wouldn't be something our parents or grandparents would have been encouraged to do.

On the plus side, we've got many new and alternative options to make more money. We've got side hustles, remote work, digital careers and opportunities that our parents couldn't even imagine. What comes with this though, is uncertainty, burnout and sometimes the need to take risks – something the older generations didn't really experience.

Old advice doesn't fit the new reality, which is why clinging to outdated money mindsets will not serve you today.

This isn't to say that you shouldn't listen to your parents' or grandparents' knowledge, but it *is* about recognising that times have changed, and we need to adapt. We can learn from the past, but we can't re-live it in a completely different world.

At the end of the day, whether you're working to live or living to work, money is the common theme that runs through it all.

Money makes the world go around

Money really does make the world go around. The clues are everywhere.

Think of all the times money is referenced in songs. There are two instances that have always stuck with me (I'm sure you've heard them before): 'Money, money, money, must be funny, in a rich man's world.' and 'Money makes the world go 'round, the world go 'round…'

Most people would just sing along, not really paying attention to the lyrics, but I've thought about them deeply.

Why is money 'funny in a rich man's world'? It's because the rich view money completely differently to everyone else. Money, and how they can make more of it, is like a game to them. It isn't just basic survival to rich people, like it was for me growing up and maybe you too. They're in abundance of it – they have so much of it and can easily make more. It's fun, it's a game.

As for 'money makes the world go 'round' – I believe that it really does, so why aren't more of us acting like it does? Why aren't we taught financial literacy in school? Why aren't we taught how to make more money, how to manage it, how to invest, the difference between good and bad debt?

It's never sat right with me that without money, life as we know it would not exist, yet money is still very much a taboo subject. It's seen as private, even shameful to talk about, but it's one of the only things we all have in common. Around the world, globally, money is needed for survival (perhaps with a few exceptions in the remotest inhabited areas). We all have to earn money, even the rich (despite the fact they may do it completely differently to how we were taught), and we all have to use money almost every day of our lives.

It is not shallow to want more money, and it is not shameful to talk about money. The more we share, the more we break the stigma of money being taboo, and the more we talk, the more we help each other to learn new skills when it comes to money, because we sure as hell didn't learn them in school.

I'm practising what I preach, and we're jumping right into the first step on your road to mastering your money: reviewing and improving your spending habits.

Chapter tasks

Action one: Take a few moments to figure out what money really means to you, and what limiting beliefs you feel you have towards money. Think about how you can reframe these. Write it all down.

Action two: Write down your favourite money affirmations and build them into your daily routine. Start to think about where you are on the spectrum between abundance and scarcity mindsets and how you can implement more of a balance.

Here are some positive money affirmations to help reframe your thinking:

- Money is a tool that I can use to create options in my life.
- I trust myself to make smart money decisions.
- I'm not bad with money, I'm just learning how to manage it properly.
- Opportunities to make money are all around me.
- I am in control of my money.
- Every financial setback is a lesson learned, not a failure.
- I am capable of making more money.

CHAPTER 1

GET SMART WITH SPENDING AND SAVING

IMPULSE SPENDING MUST be one of the biggest reasons people end up with bad debt. The wild part is a lot of the time we don't even realise it's happening.

We've literally all done it, haven't we? How many times have you gone into B&M for one thing and walked out with a multipack of chocolate you didn't need, a set of bedding you weren't planning on buying, and another cleaning product (acting as if your cupboard at home wasn't already full of bottles).[6] We're all friends here, you can admit it! The truth is, it's not just you. Shops are designed to tempt you into buying more than you intended, and we're now in a society where social media does the same thing – the drive to consume has become a 24/7 operation.

Impulse spending isn't just about money; it's about the emotion. Of course, money *is* very emotional. It affects our relationships, friendships, the way we view ourselves and others around us. We're told from a young age to speak up about our emotions and how we're feeling, but why don't we get told the same about money? Especially considering the two are so deeply connected?

Emotion drives a lot of our spending. That rush you feel when buying something new isn't just about the item, it's our brain chasing a rush of happiness. We comfort ourselves, reward ourselves and sometimes punish ourselves with money. Yes, it feels good in the moment, until reality sets in and we start to wonder why we even bought what we bought. Recognising this pattern, being honest with yourself about *why* you spend, and calling it out is where you start to take control.

There's *always* an emotion behind why we're spending. Think it through and you'll start to notice the pattern. Bored? Pass the time by spending. Stressed? Retail therapy. Unhappy? Buy something to cheer us up. Happy? Spend while we're on the buzz.

Now that we've noticed the patterns, it's time to become more mindful.

This isn't about saying you should never buy anything fun again. Money is *meant* to be spent, but in a world full of constant marketing to play with our emotions, mindful spending is essential. We're in control, so let's act like it! This means pausing before you tap your card and asking:

- Will I actually use this?
- Can I justify the spend?
- Am I buying this based on emotion or because it's genuinely adding value to my life?
- Will I still want this next week?

You can really tap into your own spending habits when you ask yourself these questions, and not only does it help you save money on pointless things you don't need, it also makes you feel good about the stuff you *do* buy, because it was meaningful.

Mindful spending often goes hand in hand with being a little more minimal. One isn't equal to the other, but they just make sense, together.

We live in a world that's constantly shouting, "Buy more, have more, upgrade everything!" So it's important to stop ourselves and hit the pause button.

The consumerist world we're living in has become 'mindless' in the sense that we're discouraged from examining our spending at any level deeper than 'the vibe' or 'treat yourself'. It's all about getting people to spend more, but never any thought for the person tapping the credit card.

We need to advocate for ourselves in this mindless consumerist culture we find ourselves in; even if we don't mean to stumble into it, it can happen almost automatically on social media, without our consent. They want us to buy that product, they want us to spend that money, and hey, that's marketing, but it's only right if we actually *want* to purchase it. And in order to understand that, we have to take it upon ourselves to become more mindful.

Forget about the Joneses

You've probably heard the phrase 'keeping up with the Joneses' before. I heard this phrase countless times throughout my teens, but what it means didn't really hit home until I dove into the finance world.

Keeping up with the Joneses means spending money to match the lifestyle of the people around you – neighbours, friends, colleagues, even strangers you follow on Instagram who always seem to be on holiday. It's the *silent* pressure to look like you're doing just as well as everyone else, even if you don't have the money to do so.

This mindset is louder than ever in our generation. Trying to simply 'keep up' is a losing battle. Social media has put everyone's highlight reel on display, making it way too easy to compare your everyday life to someone else's best bits. You see their new car, their designer bag, their latest reno, and suddenly your perfectly fine life feels like it's not enough.

It's scary how fast this can happen. Your feelings about your own life can completely change after a five-minute scroll on Instagram.

It's a classic, cliché example, but let's picture your neighbour pulling up in a new car (financed of course). Suddenly you're looking at your perfectly good car thinking, *maybe I need a new one*. Before you know it, you're doom-searching car finance options. Maybe you've not found yourself in such an extreme position, but whether it's a new car, or that new 'on trend' pair of trainers everyone on social media seems to have in eight different colours, most of us have seen something someone else has and decided that we need to have it too.

Constantly chasing what others have is exhausting, but more importantly it's financially draining. And honestly, it's never-ending.

There will *always* be someone with more. There will *always* be a new trend, *always* something to 'keep up with'. It really is a losing battle. You'll never run out of things to buy, or things you *want* to buy. But mindful spending means flipping the script. Instead of trying to keep up, ask yourself, *does this really matter to me? Does it align with my goals? Does this purchase bring me closer to the life I want, or just the life I think I should want because Sally next door has it?*

If the answer to even one of these questions is no, put that credit card down.

Don't give in to lifestyle creep

Lifestyle creep happens when your income goes up, and instead of saving or investing the difference, you slowly, and usually without noticing, increase your spending to match. It can often be 'keeping up with the Joneses' in disguise.

It's sneaky because it doesn't usually happen in one big leap. It's those little upgrades that sneak in and, once you've adjusted to a new level of spending, become your new 'normal'. The subtlety of this process makes it so much harder to go back, turning a pay rise into something that is necessary to maintaining your new lifestyle, until you fall into the cycle of constantly chasing pay rises in the hope that they will finally allow you to build wealth, only to have them lead to further lifestyle creep.

This is how people earning £25k and people earning £100k can both *feel* broke.

It's not always about how much you *earn*, it's about how much you *keep*.

Mindful spending is what can keep you from this downward spiral of lifestyle creep. It doesn't mean never treating yourself, but it does mean checking in with your choices. Asking those important questions: *Do I really want this, or am I just buying it because I can?* It's about consciously living within your means (not necessarily below them) in a way that still feels good, aligns with your goals and keeps the joy in your life.

The less pressure you put on yourself to upgrade your lifestyle, the more money and options you will have to actually live the life *you* want – not the one Instagram tells you to want.

Do what you love, not what society loves

We can get so caught up in what society deems as 'normal' and necessary that we forget what we actually want for ourselves. Over the years, with trends and virality, things that were once 'not normal' have now become normal.

When I was growing up, flash cars were a bit of a rarity. Having a BMW, Audi, Land Rover, Mercedes, meant you were *rich* rich. These cars were symbols of wealth.

Today, almost every third car you see on the road is one of those cars. It's become the norm to have one, and the truth is it's not hard to get one. They're no longer the symbol of wealth they once were, because people just stick them on finance! Society has normalised owning these expensive cars, and with that comes pressure: if everyone else has one, you feel you *should* too, otherwise you start to feel like you're falling behind.

It's the same with weddings. I honestly think wedding spending has gotten out of hand. Hen do's abroad, weddings abroad, week-long celebrations, and spending tens of thousands of pounds, often on finance. I'm not saying it's wrong to want a big wedding, if that's your dream. But the question to ask is: *is it what* you *want, or is it what society has told you is the normal way to do it?* If you've always dreamed of a lavish destination wedding and it's important to you, amazing. But if you're only doing it because everyone else is, then that's a problem.

Another example of lavish spending that has become normalised is today's expensive drinking culture. I could never justify paying £10 or more for a single cocktail now just because its presentation is 'Insta-worthy'. Don't get me wrong, I fell for this in my younger years – I've got the Insta pics to prove it. But I learned pretty quickly that I wasn't actually enjoying it. I was doing it for the picture, in that hope that people would think *look at her living her best life,* and not for myself.

My intention here isn't to shame you or anyone else. It's your money, and if it brings you genuine joy, spend it. What I want to hit home is this: *spend on what you love, not what society has convinced you that you love.*

When you strip away the pressure, the comparisons, the 'keeping up' mentality, and you actually sit with yourself and ask, *what do I really value?,* that's when your spending starts to feel good. That's when money becomes a tool for *your* happiness, not someone else's highlight reel that you feel caught up in.

When you start to filter out what society tells you to spend on and focus only on what actually matters to you, you'll notice that a lot of your purchases aren't urgent, or even necessary at all. They don't need to be made in the heat of the moment, on an impulse thought. They don't need to be 'because everyone else is doing it'. Sometimes, the best thing you can do for yourself (and your bank balance) is just pause. Sit with it. Ask yourself those important questions and figure out if the thing you're planning to spend on is *really* what you want, whether it aligns with your spending goals and – most importantly – whether it aligns with your joy.

Try out the 24-hour rule

Something I absolutely swear by is the 24-hour rule. This rule is for when you've hit that pause button and you're unsure how you feel about whatever it is you're thinking about buying. You know it's not a *need*, it's more of a *want* item, and you're not entirely sure if you should buy it.

Take a photo of the item (or write down what it is on a 'wants list') and re-visit it after 24 hours. If you still feel like you want to buy it, and it'll bring you joy or add value to your life, then go ahead. Trust me, more often than not, you'll be completely over the item 24 hours later. Sometimes you'll even forget about it completely.

The beauty of this rule is that it gives you space to make a decision without the emotional high of being in the moment. Impulse buys often happen because we're running off the dopamine hit from seeing something new or finding something that our favourite influencer told us we *must* get. Waiting a day lets your logical brain catch up with your emotional brain, and you'll be surprised how often the urge disappears.

Sabotage yourself

Implementing something like the 24-hour rule can be hard if you're a serial impulse spender, but there are other handy little things you can do to hit that pause button. For example, you *sabotage yourself* (it sounds weird, but future-you will thank present-you for this one).

Create little barriers between you and your spending that make it harder to act on impulse. They might sound small, but trust me, they can add up when it comes to savings.

Here are some of my favourite minor inconveniences that can actually stop you from spending money:

- **Don't save your card details**: or you can even delete them from your most-used sites. Honestly, this works wonders. It sounds tiny, but having to physically get up and find your bank card gives you that extra pause to think *do I really need this?* I've done this myself, and often I'm too lazy to get up off the sofa and so decide the purchase is not worth it. I never regret it and have never once ended up missing the thing I almost bought.
- **Delete the apps**: if you know you can't scroll ASOS or Amazon without filling a basket, take them off your home screen, or delete them altogether for a while. Break the habit! Out of sight, out of mind does work wonders.
- **Unsubscribe from marketing emails**: those sale emails are designed to make you feel like you're missing out (you're not, by the way). Unsubscribing reduces the temptation before it even hits you.
- **Make your money less instant**: it's so easy to spend money in our day and age! If you use Apple Pay or Google Pay, consider removing your card. Again, having to physically reach for your wallet adds just enough inconvenience to stop a mindless tap.

Think of these little inconveniences as speed bumps. They don't stop you from ever spending (because spending is fine when it's intentional) but they slow you down long enough to check in with your mindful spending brain.

Little habits like the 24-hour rule all play a part in the bigger picture – the budgeting picture. Now, before you roll your eyes (budgeting gets a bad rep because it's commonly confused with being restrictive, which it really is not), understand that budgeting is not about constantly saying no in order to 'stick to your budget'. It's actually about knowing where your money is going, instead of just *wondering* where it went. It's about you being in control and making room with your money for the things that matter rather than losing money on things that don't.

Make peace with budgeting

A budget is like your money's own sat nav, telling it where to go. Without a budget, money just slips through your fingers and you don't even notice it happening.

We've covered impulse spending and wondering where our money went, but if we maintain a budget *we never have to wonder* where our money went, because we already know!

A budget doesn't *stop* you from spending, it simply manages *how* we're spending. It's a plan for our money that gives us clarity, control and, most importantly, confidence that when we spend we know it's money we have got. This helps us avoid those purchases coming back to bite us later on.

So where does the sat nav come into it? You know where you want your money to go, whether that's a holiday, paying off debt or just not stressing near the end of the month. A budget maps out the route. Without it, you're basically driving in circles – spending, spending, spending with no view on how much is left – and hoping you'll end up somewhere good (and that you'll make it to your next pay day).

Spoiler alert: it never ends well.

With that money sat nav, you know every turn, every stop (every pound spent, when and why) and even have space for detours (because you're planning for your treats).

It's quite scary how many people I've spoken with that don't check their bank account transactions. They don't know how much money is coming in or going out, and they end up dipping into their savings or overdraft before reaching their next pay day.

Checking your bank balance regularly, even before taking the step of creating a budget, is the first step to taking control of your money.

This is where I like to have a weekly 'money date' with myself. Yes, I romanticise these things, because why not?

Picture this: picking your drink of choice, sitting down all cosy and checking those transactions. It's bliss. Seriously, it becomes that enjoyable!

Or maybe that's just me, but you won't know unless you try it.

Knowing what comes into your bank account and what goes out of it gives you so much more mental clarity around your money and finances. Those weekly money dates are essential for that clarity.

Before we continue with more budgeting tips, I want to detour briefly to discuss a mental model that works brilliantly for establishing where you are on your financial education journey. We'll then use this model to help establish our budgeting sat nav.

Get clued up with the conscious unconscious competence model

I first came across this model when I worked in learning and development, and it's stuck with me ever since because it really is relevant to every part of new learning in life, especially when it comes to money. I love how it really captures the stages of learning anything new. It's especially helpful when you feel useless at something, because that is literally the *first step* towards getting better. You might feel clueless at this point because you're now aware of your money, but you're not sure where to go from here.

That's why I love this model when it comes to money. It shows you that not knowing, messing up and feeling clueless are all perfectly normal. These feelings and failures are all just part of the process. As you can see from the image below, the model plots the route from incompetence to competence in any field, breaking this down into four stages.

The conscious/unconscious competence model

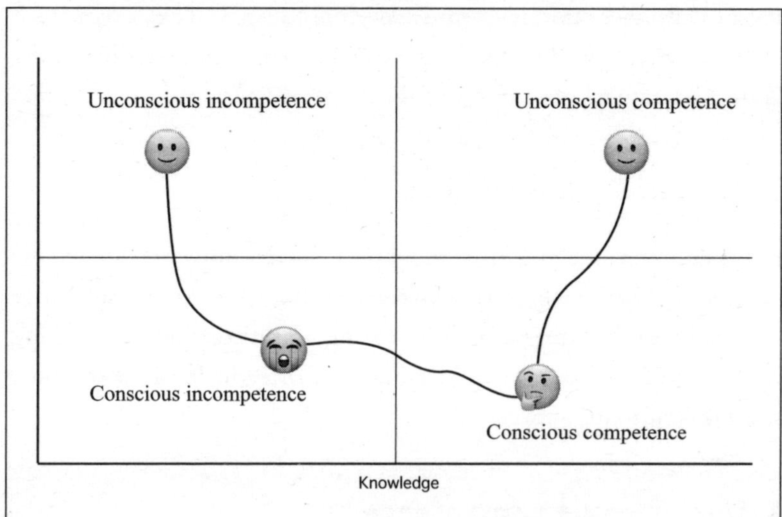

Here's how the model works when it comes to money, taking it from the first stage to the last:

1. Unconscious incompetence

You don't know what you don't know.

At this stage, you're blissfully unaware. Maybe you're spending, getting by, not even realising you're making money mistakes. You don't know there's a better way because you don't even know the problem exists (you might find yourself thinking things like *erm where's all my money going?* but not digging any deeper, just waiting for your next pay day and then repeating the process next month).

2. Conscious incompetence

You now know that you don't know.

You've now become aware that you're lacking a certain skill or ability, and this can feel uncomfortable, but it gives you the motivation to want to improve. You realise you're overspending, you can't keep track of bills or that your debt has become out of hand, but you don't really know how to get yourself out of the situation.

3. Conscious competence

You're now learning and applying, but it's a big effort.

This is where you start actively learning how to manage your money. You're building a budget, setting up savings pots or tracking your spending. It doesn't feel natural yet, though. It's a lot of effort and takes thinking power.

4. Unconscious competence

It becomes second nature.

Your habits are now on autopilot. They're cemented into your brain. You've learned the skill so well, you don't even have to think about it anymore. It's just part of your life. This is when you're now spending mindfully, without having to micro-manage every penny. It just happens.

Apply the model to budgeting and money

When you first start taking control of your money, and when you tackle budgeting in particular, you'll probably feel a bit clueless. You'll wonder if you're doing it right, or you'll forget to update things, or you'll spend from a pot that was saved for something else. This is you sitting in *conscious incompetence* and moving towards *conscious competence.*

The trick is to push through those stages, knowing that the

more you practise, the easier it becomes. Eventually, budgeting and managing money stops feeling like hard work and starts becoming effortless and, as I told you, even enjoyable!

The goal is to reach *unconscious competence* with your money. To have saving, budgeting and mindful spending feel as natural as possible.

Find a budget that works for you

So, let's talk budgeting. And let's get one thing straight: you are not *on* a budget; you *have* a budget. There's a *big* difference. The language you use matters. You're on a budget? Sounds restrictive. You have a budget? Sounds like you're in control!

There's no one way to budget, and that's why budgeting isn't boring, restrictive or confusing, because we have to find what works for *you*, and if it works for you and your lifestyle, you'll actually enjoy having your budget.

Going back to our lovely sat nav: just like when you type an address into a navigation app, there's usually more than one route. Some are faster, some longer, some avoid toll roads. Budgeting works the same way.

Here are some of the most popular budgeting routes:

- **The 50/30/20 rule**: 50% of your income goes on needs, 30% on wants, 20% on savings or debt. Now, I'm not too much of a fan of this method, but it can work for a lot of people. It's simple, it's methodical, it's easy to calculate.
- **Zero-based budgeting**: every pound gets assigned to be spent on something specific (or saved). This is the budgeting method I use, because it's quite flexible while still knowing where all of your money goes. It means you're left with zero by the next pay day,

because you've planned where every pound is going. Essentially, it's the formula: income – expenses – savings = 0.

- **Pay yourself first**: instead of saving what's left over (there's usually nothing left), you put money into savings or investments first and then live on the rest. This is very fluid and still doesn't really manage the majority of your money that's left over after saving, but it's a great stepping stone to give your money some direction and ensures you're prioritising your savings goal.
- **Envelope/cash stuffing/pots system**: cash envelopes are an old-school method that some people still love. Some people find having physical cash is much easier to budget with. You can use the same method digitally if you use a bank that has 'pots'. This is where you split your money into categories so you can literally see what's left for each area.

The best one to choose is: whatever works best for you. The magic isn't actually in the method, it's in the consistency.

Pick a route, stick with it for a while, and if it doesn't feel right, try a different one. It's all trial and error, until you find the right fit for you. If you don't try to find what works for you, trust me that money will keep disappearing, and you'll be left wondering where it went every month.

If you're thinking, *but Meg, how do I actually start, help me out, I've not done this before!* I got you! Here's a simple step-by-step guide to establishing your budgeting baseline so that you can pick your preferred budgeting method. We're not going to get carried away with this, but we can start to add the trickier things like irregular costs once we get the gist (don't worry, we'll cover these soon too).

Step 1: Know your numbers

Write down your take-home pay. To the penny, what you actually receive each month, because I bet you don't know off the top of your head. Not "I get paid around £1,600 a month" – we need £1627.59! We need the exact figure.

Step 2: Identify your bare bones items

Rent/mortgage, council tax, gas/electric, water, transport, childcare, phone, insurance. These are your fixed bills. Bills that you have to pay whether you like it or not. (We'll call this your 'bare bones' budget: how much money you need to live and survive.)

Step 3: Factor in groceries and life basics

Decide how much you'll set aside for food, fuel and essentials. Keep it realistic. You can easily get a base for this by checking your spending in these categories on your banking app over previous months. You can also connect budgeting apps such as Snoop to your bank accounts to categorise your spending, so you can easily find out how much you're spending and where.

Step 4: Set aside some fun money

Give yourself a little pot of fun money for things like coffees, meals out, treats. This is important because we don't want your budget to start to feel restrictive. Life is for living, money is for enjoying. Let's make room for the things that bring us joy, sensibly.

Step 5: Check the balance

Add it all up. Does it fit within your take-home pay? If not, start to adjust your categories. Start with your wants before needs.

Step 6: Set it up

On pay day, move the money into separate pots based on the budgeting method you want to try (many banking apps let you do this) or simply mentally assign that money to your categories (e.g., one for bills, one for groceries, one for fun). That way, you can easily see what's left.

Step 7: Weekly (or monthly) money date

I know you're getting excited at the thought of that cosy money date with your fave cuppa! Spend ten minutes once a week looking at your money and what's left. This is where you'll start to see what's working and what may need adjusting for next month.

That's it. You now have a working budget. It wasn't that scary, was it? Keep it simple for your first month or two, and once you've nailed the basics you can start to add additional categories, unexpected spends, events like birthdays, Christmas and, most importantly, your emergency fund!

Add flavour with these practical tips

I'm throwing in some bonus practical tips to help your budget thrive, because I want this budget to succeed for you as much as you do!

These are small things that have helped me along the way when it came to successful budgeting:

- Try to have all of your bills go out on the same day, or at least in the same week. You can easily change this with your providers. It's much more visually appealing on your banking app when all of your big bills are sorted and what's left can be assigned to your non-fixed bills such as food shopping, fuel and fun!
- Rename your savings pots with your goals. Instead of 'savings', call it 'holiday fund' or 'house deposit' – I know I bang on about it, but visualising things makes them so much more real. Knowing you're about to dip into your 'house savings' pot makes you not want to do it; it makes it more emotional, more meaningful than a pot called 'savings' which has no visual destination.
- Automate as much as possible. Technology has advanced so much, let's use it to our advantage. We can now automate our savings and move bills over to different accounts without having to think about it. We don't need to rely on our own willpower or memory. Let's make life easier for ourselves.
- Leave a small buffer in your current account, even just £20–£30. This avoids the stress of accidentally going overdrawn or dipping into savings if you do end up having a budgeting malfunction or an impulse spend (because yes, they will still happen).

Make it fun with spending challenges

Budgeting can sometimes feel a bit dry (not for me, I love it!) and if you're someone who likes a little excitement, that can make it harder to stick with. This is where *spending challenges* can help you.

These are like little games you play with your money to keep things exciting, give yourself a goal and help you build the habit of saying no in a way that feels fun rather than restrictive.

Now, spending challenges don't work for everyone! For some, they can feel too restrictive and backfire. But for others, they're an amazing way to reframe money habits and keep things interesting. I'm not here to tell you there's only one way to budget. I'm here to give you the tools so you can pick what works for *you*.

Here are some popular spending challenges you could try:

- **No-spend day**: pick one day a week where you commit to spending absolutely nothing (apart from essentials). That means no morning coffee, no grabbing a meal deal, no Amazon orders. It can help you realise just how much you *don't* need to spend.
- **No-frills weekend**: instead of heading out for meals, drinks or shopping, find free or low-cost activities: movie nights at home, park walks, cooking challenges with what's already in your cupboards. This pushes you to get creative while saving money.
- **Low-spend weeks**: rather than cutting yourself off completely, set yourself a small spending allowance for the week and challenge yourself to stick to it.
- **Buy nothing new**: for a whole month, commit to something like only buying second-hand or shopping your own wardrobe to use what you already own. This is a good one if you're a serial shopper.

You might read these and think *absolutely not*, and that's okay. If I'm honest, I'm not a fan of spending challenges either, but I'd be doing you a disservice by not mentioning them, because they work amazingly for some.

The idea of these challenges isn't to restrict yourself forever, it's about experimenting with different ways of saying no, so you build confidence in your ability to stick to your budget. You might find one you absolutely love that can become part of your monthly routine.

Pay yourself first

I feel like I say this a lot about money habits, but the 'pay yourself first' approach changed the game for me, and so it deserves its own little section in this book. If you didn't really see the appeal when it was mentioned just a couple of pages ago, I aim to convince you about this game changer now.

Here's the important bit:

Don't save what is left after spending, spend what is left after saving.

It's such a simple concept that when I first learned about it, I thought *why didn't I think of this myself?* I couldn't believe I had to be told! When you pay yourself first, your savings are *always* prioritised. A lot of us do the reverse, trying to save after spending, near the end of the month (I'm not ashamed to admit that I used to do this), and guess what? Most of the time it fails because there is never anything left to save.

How many of us get to the end of the month with no money left and think *I guess I'll try and save next month*?

I used to think *why can't I save? Where is my money even going?* These are questions a lot of people ask themselves. The truth is, often the problem isn't that you don't have any money to save, it's that the order in which you're saving needs to be re-jigged.

We spend because the money is there, so what if the money isn't there? It's not a trick question: we obviously can't spend it! That's why it's important to pay ourselves first. You can't spend what isn't there, but the beauty is that it hasn't gone on new clothes or some extra food shopping – it's in your savings, building up!

We all make sure we pay our mortgage provider, our landlord, our energy provider. We prioritise these people (who are mostly faceless corporations) and make sure they're paid. We wouldn't dare spend *their* money, so why not prioritise ourselves, our own goals and our future by paying ourselves first too?

Building this habit helped me to save thousands in my 20s. I decided to pay myself first, and that was when saving became easier.

Stick to your budget

Making a budget is the easy part. Sticking to it is the hard bit (although it doesn't *have* to be hard). A budget only works if you stay consistent.

Tap into your money mindset, know your own spending triggers and equip yourself with an emergency fund (just wait, we're almost there) and savings pots to stay prepared for anything.

Typical spending triggers can include:

- **Emotional spending**: shopping when stressed, sad, or even happy.
- **Boredom scrolling**: online shopping to fill time.
- **Sales and discounts**: buying something just because it's on offer.
- **Peer pressure**: friends persuading you to go out or spend more than you planned.
- **Special occasions**: birthdays, weddings, nights out (when you didn't plan for it).

Once you know your triggers, you can start putting things in place to stop them taking over, like those minor inconveniences we spoke about earlier, whether that's unsubscribing from marketing emails, deleting apps or simply giving yourself the 24-hour pause before buying.

Aim for *progress*, not *perfect*

I want you to remember that it's taken me years to build my money habits, and months to perfect my budget. Even now, it still has curveballs thrown at it! Kids, house moves, unexpected bills, the cost of living itself – sometimes the budget just goes out the window (and that's okay. It's all part of the journey). What matters is that you *start*, and then you keep moving forward. Progress, not perfection, is what will change your money story. I never tell my kids that practice makes perfect. I tell them that practice makes progress. We need to strive to learn and do better, rather than trying to hit the destination of perfection (which by the way, doesn't exist).

Consider an emergency fund

Having an emergency fund will change your life.

No, I'm not being dramatic.

You may think an emergency fund is overkill if you've already got a savings pot. Surely you don't need a savings pot, and then another savings pot purely for emergencies? Or maybe you're wondering *what the hell is an emergency fund?* Either way, let me see if I can sell you the idea.

What is an emergency fund?

An emergency fund – much like it says on the tin – is a pot of money that you build up for emergencies only. I'm not talking about when you have no money left in the budget and you want to grab a coffee, I'm talking losing your job unexpectedly, having to pay yourself for a few months while finding another job, the car breaking down a week before Christmas, your MOT failing, your dishwasher leaking. Something that is so unplanned, you're not expecting the expense in your monthly budget. Your emergency fund is prepared for whatever comes up and prevents you having to dip into your house savings, holiday savings, overdraft, credit card or whatever pot of money would otherwise foot the bill.

It happens. I can count many occasions where an unexpected expense has cropped up that would cripple my usual monthly budget if I didn't have my emergency fund in place.

Why do you need one?

My finances are under much better control since I implemented an emergency fund in my budget. Those inconveniences that pop up no longer feel as inconvenient or as major, because I am prepared for the unexpected.

Imagine losing your job, and just knowing you have three, four or even six months' worth of expenses saved in your emergency fund, ready for this moment. Think of the stress it would relieve. Compared to the stress, panic and fear you'd feel if you didn't have any of this money saved.

It literally takes an 'ahhhhh!' moment and changes it to a 'mehh' moment.

Knowing you can handle unexpected things without needing to panic will bring you serious peace of mind. Not just that, it also gives you freedom. You can choose to get out of that job that's causing you mental health problems, take a break for a month or two until you find something better.

I hope you never (or realistically, rarely) need to dip into your emergency fund. But I can promise you that it is better to have it and not need it, than to need it and not have it.

Why does it specifically need to be an 'emergency fund'?

You can organise your finances however works best for you, but as I've mentioned before, visualisation can really help you to compartmentalise your finances. Giving your savings a name and a purpose helps you to stick to your goal and only use that pot as you initially intended.

So let's picture this: you have a 'new house' savings pot, you *don't* have an emergency fund. Your car fails its MOT and you need £400 worth of repairs. Your choices? Borrow the money from somewhere or someone. Taking it out of that new house savings pot will hit you right in the emotions, because you know that money was supposed to go towards your new home, but now it's going on your car. This is demoralising *and* inconvenient.

Let's flip the script: you have an emergency fund. That £400 was instantly taken from it. Your new house savings are still intact. You don't feel as wounded, as that's what your emergency fund is there for. The situation doesn't feel like such a major inconvenience. Everyone's happy.

I know you're probably already sold and want to run to your online banking app to set up your emergency fund, but before you do that, let's look at how much you should put into that emergency fund, and how you can actually start to build one.

The magic number

"How much do I need to save in my emergency fund?" is *the* question everyone asks when setting one up. But the truth is that there *is* no magic number for your emergency fund.

As a general rule of thumb, enough to cover three-to-six months of essential outgoings is a great number to aim for. It's a good buffer against the worst-case scenario of losing your job, since that amount of time will generally be enough for you to find other work.

There are also emergency fund calculators you can access with a simple Google search that can help you to find *your* perfect amount.

If you're thinking *oh my gosh, I can't save that much* – look, it's a process, start building up one month to begin with, then go for two, then so on. Having something is better than nothing.

Let's get building

This is why getting to grips with your budget comes before anything else: we need the foundations of your budget to start building your emergency fund.

First, we're going to need the sum total of the outgoings that you wrote down for your budget:

Want three months' worth of expenses in your emergency fund? Multiply that number by three.

Want four months' worth of expenses in your emergency fund? Multiply that number by four.

Want five months' worth of… you get the gist!

You'll then have the number you need in your emergency fund to feel comfortable knowing that anything unexpected can happen and you'll be just fine.

So now you know your number, how do you get to it? You might be thinking *sh**t, how can I save* that *much money?*

Well, you start small.

Whether you can afford to put £10, £20 or £50 into that emergency fund each month, you stick to it. Like everything, consistency is key. Those small amounts add up.

Let's maintain your emergency fund

Maintaining your fund is all about consistency – keeping the habit going. Here's how we're going to make it stick:

1. **Automate your monthly contribution**: treat it like a bill. Set it up as an automatic payment. Out of sight, out of mind.
2. **Top it up with extra, unexpected money**: if you receive birthday money, an unexpected tax refund, or your monthly bills decrease, use that extra money towards your emergency fund.

3. **Review every few months**: be sure to check in. If you're feeling the pinch in your budget, decrease your contribution. Feel like you could be adding more? Increase it. It's all adding to that overall target.
4. **Only use it for true emergencies**: not for treats. This fund is your safety net.
5. **Celebrate milestones**: even if just internally, celebrate your achievements.

It's not about how fast you can build it; it's about having something there rather than nothing. Build the habit, keep it consistent. You owe yourself the peace of mind that comes from knowing that when life throws unexpected things at you, you'll be ready for them.

Test the water with sinking funds

Savings pots and sinking funds are essentially the same thing. I want to get you up to date with the money lingo. I've mentioned savings pots a few times, but a lot of the time they're referred to as sinking funds.

It was only a few years back that I seriously implemented sinking funds into my financial management, and they were another game changer. (I feel like I say almost everything is a game changer, but it's because so many of these little habits, tools and methods to get your money in check really are!)

You've got your budget in place, you've got your emergency fund building up nicely, you might even have a general savings pot for nothing specific, and then you have your sinking funds. These are for non-emergency things but are quite specific. Things that you like to be prepared for like buying birthday gifts, a treat-yourself fund, a Christmas pot (so you can save all year bit by bit).

By now you know that I'm a big fan of visualisation, and just like your emergency fund, the reason why we use sinking funds is to make your savings more visual. Everything needs its place and purpose – and giving your money a purpose helps you to spend it with intention and without guilt.

Knowing that your treat-yourself fund exists so that you can get your nails done, book a spa day, get your hair cut, *empowers* you to do those things without guilt, rather than feeling bad for dipping into your savings.

That birthday fund will keep you afloat when you have three birthdays to buy for in one month. Before you created your sinking fund, this kind of thing would feel like it had crept up on you, and trying to find extra cash when you may not have it could be really stressful.

Think about the things that you may end up spending money on that leave you with that tight feeling near the end of the month – whether that's treats for yourself, social events, the kids' activities. You can set up your sinking funds for whatever you need help spending on with intention and guilt-free.

Break free with an f-you fund

I wanted to give a moment to the ever-so-popular f***-you fund. We kept it PG up there with our sensible emergency fund, but the f-you fund might suit you better if you want just a little more freedom.

Think of this as the unhinged version of an emergency fund. While your emergency fund is there to protect you from life's curveballs (boilers breaking, cars dying, jobs being cut), your f-you fund is there to protect you from people. Protecting you from situations, bosses or relationships where you feel trapped purely because you need the money.

If you've ever sat in a job you hate, biting your tongue because you couldn't afford to lose that income, or listened to a boss you can't stand because you know you've got bills to pay, you might just benefit from the f-you fund. It's the pot of money that gives you options. The money that lets you walk away without any fear. The money that allows you to put yourself, your values and your mental health first, rather than always choosing the security of other money, purely because you have no choice.

The difference:

- Emergency fund = safety net for unexpected life events.
- F-you fund = freedom fund for when you've simply had enough.

For me, I like to think of the f-you fund as a little pot of financial independence. You've bought yourself the right to say, "F-you, no!" when something doesn't serve you.

Decide where to save

The chances of you still being with the bank your mum set up your first account with when you were 13 are high, because why change? It's easy to stick to what you've always known. For a long time, I was the same. My first ever bank account was with Halifax, and guess what? I still have an account with Halifax (for good reason), but let me tell you, who you bank with, or more importantly, who you *save* with, matters.

You might be thinking, *you've told me to budget, you've told me to set up savings pots and an emergency fund, but where can I open up all these things?*

Don't worry, I've got you.

Different accounts have different benefits, different levels of flexibility, and different interest rates (aka how much money your savings can earn).

Digital pots

A lot of banks now let you create digital 'pots' inside your account. These are like mini accounts where you can split up your money for different goals (these are what people like to use for their sinking funds).

The two favourite banks among my savvy community are Chase and Monzo. Both have really user-friendly apps and offer additional handy features to stay in check with your money – like spending insights. Your current bank may have something similar, as more and more banks are taking this modern approach to handling money, so if you like the sound of these benefits but don't want to switch to a new bank, you may not have to.

Types of accounts

Here are the main types of accounts you'll come across, and what they're used for.

Current account

This is your everyday account where your wages are paid in and bills typically go out. It's not really designed for saving, but you need one for your day-to-day spending. Some current accounts come with perks (like cashback or interest), so it's worth checking if yours is giving you anything back.

General savings account

This type of savings account is simple and flexible. You can put money in, take money out, and they usually don't have restrictions. The downside is that while you might earn a little interest while you save, the interest rates tend to be low, so your money probably won't grow much. These are best used to save for short-term goals and when you want easy access to your money.

Cash ISA (Individual Savings Account)

You don't pay tax on the interest you earn with any money you save in a cash ISA (up to your allowance of £20,000 per year, as of the 2026/27 tax year. Great if you're saving bigger amounts and want to make the most of being able to earn interest tax-free.

Lifetime ISA (LISA)

An account specifically designed for saving for your first home or retirement. You can save up to £4,000 per year, and the government gives you a 25% bonus on top! The caveat is that you can *only* use it for a house deposit or after age 60 without penalties. Restrictions do apply to house prices, so make sure you look into this before opening a LISA.

Fixed-term savings account

These lock your money away for a set period, in exchange for a higher interest rate. They're good for money you won't need access to straight away.

Premium bonds

Premium bonds are not technically a type of savings account, but they're worth a mention here. Instead of earning interest, your money goes into a prize draw where you could win tax-free cash. These are government backed, so are an extremely safe place to keep your money.

Why interest rates matter

Interest rates determine the amount your bank will pay you for keeping your money with them. This is where the savviness of shopping around for the best bank account with the highest interest rate comes in. An account with a higher interest rate means more money for you.

If one bank pays 0.5% and another pays 5%, that's literally the difference between your £1,000 earning you an additional £5 in a year and £50 in a year. It's not much, but it all adds up, and I'd much rather get £50 than £5, wouldn't you?

This isn't just for your personal money either; you can shop around for business accounts if you're self-employed or a business owner. I only recently swapped my business money into a saver account because it was earning 0% interest. Now I'm earning over 3.5%, which is better late than never, but I should have definitely moved it earlier. Like I said though, nobody's perfect, and I'm still learning!

How many accounts should I have?

So how many bank accounts should you have? As with so much in personal finance, there's no right or wrong answer to this. But that said, you should have at least two.

Many people have only one bank account for almost everything, until they start taking control of their money. They have their salary going in, their bills coming out *and* their day-to-day spending all coming out of that same account. When everything's coming in and out of one account, it can get messy, confusing and a tad overwhelming. That's why I always recommend having a separate bank account for your day-to-day spending.

Here's how I'd recommend starting:

- **Current account one:** salary gets paid in, bills come out. These are fixed bills such as rent, energy, council tax, water, Wi-Fi and so on. All of these bills get paid out soon after pay day and as near to each other as possible, either on the same day or in the same week, so you know everything's paid for and done for that month.
- **Current account two:** this is where day-to-day spending comes from. Transfer money you've budgeted for general spending from current account one to current account two – this is for things like food shopping, fuel, days out.

Splitting things like this just makes spending and money feel a lot calmer. You don't have to keep an eye on your balance, worrying about accidentally spending money that is meant for an important bill, because it's in its own account, with a purpose. Then you've got your spending account, which feels a bit more guilt-free, because you know it's already been budgeted for. It just takes away that messy, overwhelming feeling and gives you a bit more peace of mind! It's honestly such a simple solution which provides so much more clarity.

This is a good starting point, and from here you can keep it as simple or as complex as you like. You may already have multiple accounts open, or you may want to start opening others for savings goals or sinking funds.

Now you have the real core elements of your financial future lined up, let's look at some next-level money management: turning spending *into* saving.

Chapter tasks

Action one: Think about what it is that you really want from your money, what matters to you. Do you get caught up in social media and societal norms? Take time to figure out how you can be more mindful when it comes to spending.

Action two: Open up your calendar and set yourself a money date. This is where you'll officially start planning your budget.

Action three: Figure out your emergency fund number, open up a separate savings account and set up your standing order of whatever amount you can afford to start up your emergency fund.

Action four: If you currently have a savings pot, check the interest rate and shop around for better interest rates to make sure you're getting the most for your money.

Action five: Take a look at your current money set-up and see if you think opening an additional bank account could help you manage your money more efficiently.

CHAPTER 2

SAVE AS YOU SPEND

YOU PROBABLY THINK I'm exaggerating if I say that I save money every time I spend (okay, it's *almost* every time I spend).

There seems to be a general consensus that saving money is boring and that it must make you miserable because you're always obsessively pinching pennies. People also assume that saving money means cutting back on the things you enjoy.

This couldn't be further from the truth.

I've said it before, and I'll say it again: life is for living, and when it comes to money, everything is about balance. Sometimes this means that while you're spending on the things that you love, you can also put a little away for a rainy day.

Live, laugh, love below your means

Hearing the phrase 'live below your means' makes me roll my eyes a little bit these days. It's used excessively in the finance world as a shorthand for stooping to any level necessary to achieve your goals. It sounds horrible, and has become a proper finance cliché alongside cancelling Netflix, never buying takeaway coffee, and not even dreaming about avocado toast. The message behind all of these tropes is, basically, if you want to save money you need to live as simply as humanly possible until you retire.

Who wants that? Not me, and I doubt you do either.

Here's the truth: living below your means doesn't mean sucking all the joy out of your life. It simply means making sure the life you're living is sustainable, and that your spending doesn't constantly outpace what's coming in. Most importantly, it means being mindful of your cash flow. The reason behind this is simple: if you're always at the edge of your income, one unexpected bill or hiccup can knock *everything* off balance.

The real danger is actually *lifestyle creep*. You start earning more, and instead of that extra income working for you, it just quietly gets spent on little upgrades. You start ordering more takeaways. Buying more clothes. Maybe you upgrade your car, your phone, your gym, your holidays, all without even thinking about it... Before you know it, that bigger income feels just as tight as the old one did. You're still stressed, and *still living paycheck to paycheck*.

Here's the mindset shift you need (because we know how important your mindset is by this point: living below your means doesn't have to mean *sacrificing*. It's about being *intentional* with your spending and getting as much as you can from each transaction. You can still enjoy takeaways, holidays, meals out, and the things that you enjoy, but you're doing it in a way that fits your bigger money picture.

You really can cut your everyday expenses *without* sacrificing living. You can still go out for meals, have fun days out, buy yourself new clothes when you need them without feeling like you're breaking the bank. (Sometimes you can even do these things for free, but we'll talk about that when we get into side hustles.)

Would you believe me if I told you that our household has a takeaway twice a week, and we *never* pay full price for it? It actually pains me that other people are paying full price when there's no need to.

The secret? Well, there's actually more than one, and they're not even secret.

Cashback. Discount codes. Offers. These things are available to *everyone*, yet so many people don't even know they exist or think to use them!

Let's start with cashback. I've been using cashback sites to save money for over a decade, and I've saved thousands. It's putting money back in your own pocket, by essentially offering you part of your money back after buying something.

You wouldn't turn that down now, would you?

Claim your cash back with... cashback

You can basically get cashback on anything. Your grocery shopping, at restaurants, takeaways, insurance policies, clothes, holidays, days out.

Cashback sites work in partnership with countless different retailers that we all know and love (ASOS, Amazon, Asda, Morrisons – just to name a few). When we shop with the retailer via the cashback site, the cashback site gets a commission from the retailer for giving them a customer – and the cashback site is lovely enough to share that commission with you.

Some people ask me, "but why would they do that?" Well, why wouldn't they? It's a win-win for everybody. The retailer gets a customer, the cashback site makes some money, and *you* save some money.

It gets better too. There are so many cashback sites these days that they all compete with each other to give you the best cashback rate. Sometimes you can get as high as 10% or 12% back on your food shopping at somewhere like Asda.

You can keep up to date with the best cashback sites and apps by following me on social media, but at the time of writing this, my top few favourites are:

- TopCashback
- Everup
- Quidco
- Jam Doughnut

These sites are UK-specific, but wherever you are in the world you should have cashback sites you can use. Who knows, maybe some of these will have gone global by the time you read this.

Cashback is literally the key to cutting your expenses without sacrificing the things you enjoy. You'll be saving on the things you already spend money on, which leaves more money to go out for more meals, enjoy more days out, or even simply save more money for your future goals.

People really underestimate the difference using cashback can make. Imagine being able to save £10–£50 extra every month (conservatively). I mean, the amount of cashback you earn depends on how much you spend, but even just on groceries alone it's not hard to save £10 a month purely from cashback. If you can't afford to save any money at the end of the month because you're spending everything you earn, cashback can give you the means to take that first crucial step into saving.

Don't sleep on it.

I'm spending so long on cashback because I honestly love it so much. If a random stranger in the street offered you a £10 note, you'd be pleased with that, right? This is the attitude you need to have about cashback.

Note: some cashback sites do sometimes sneak in a monthly fee for the privilege of signing up to their websites – none of the websites I recommend, or any you sign up to should ask for a monthly fee. (Caveat: TopCashback is one of my favourite cashback websites; they have two membership options currently: a free version and a plus version – they deduct £5 annually from the cashback you've made on the site, this is OPTIONAL.)

Never pay full price if you can avoid it

Let's not forget discount codes and offers. With the helping hand of AI, it's easier than ever to find discount codes whenever you're shopping. Simply ask your favourite AI if they can find you a discount code for whatever retailer it is you're shopping with, and it'll usually find one in seconds. I never shop online without searching for a discount code first. Sometimes it doesn't pay off, but at least I've tried to save money. Most the time, though, I find a discount code that works.

There are sites out there like VoucherCodes that showcase discount codes and offers, and even compensate you if a code no longer works. Checking sites like this needs to become one of your online shopping habits.

You might be thinking that all this sounds like a lot of effort – but it only takes an extra few minutes, and once you build it into a habit, it becomes second nature.

I'm sure you've heard the cliched saying, 'look after the pennies and the pounds take care of themselves' – well this is my motto when it comes to cashback and using discounts. It all adds up. Don't sleep on those small amounts you can save, because over months and years they can amount to a huge pile of money.

I've had members of my savvy community fund their whole Christmas from cashback they've earnt over the year, and even people funding holidays abroad from money they've saved. It sounds dramatic, but that really is life-changing stuff.

Let small habits make a big difference

When it comes to money, it's the tiny habits we keep up consistently that make the biggest difference.

Let's compare saving money to brushing your teeth before bed. You don't brush once for ten minutes and then stop for the rest of the week; you brush every day for two minutes, and this small, consistent habit keeps your teeth healthy. In the same way, saving small amounts consistently can keep your finances looking healthy.

Small habits never feel life changing in the moment, of course, but it's about the momentum you build up to create consistent changes that lead to the big differences. Using cashback sites and discount codes is just the same.

Let me tell you a figure that shocks me every time I hear it.

£27.50 a day.

If you were to spend £27.50 a day for a year, that adds up to over £10,000 in total. When I've shared this figure before, I've had the response "but who's spending £27.50 a day?"

Let me show you how easy it is to spend £27.50 a day:

- Public transport to and from work: £7
- Coffee on your way to work: £4.20
- Lunch meal deal: £3.75
- Stop off on the way home to grab dinner: £12

Anyway, it's not about how easy it is to spend that amount every day, or whether anybody actually does spend that amount per day – it's about how such a small amount can equal such a substantial figure over a period of time. This works both ways, with how you spend and how you save. Let this stick with you when it comes to everyday savings, because it really does all add up.

Pay those bills, your way

Now let's talk about something that drains a huge amount of our money but we can't get rid – even though we'd love to: bills and food shopping. These are the two biggest household costs after rent or a mortgage, so if you can get savvy here, you'll feel the difference.

Here are some quick-fire tips you can implement fast:

Bills

- **Don't be loyal**: whether for energy, broadband or mobile, loyalty costs you money. Set a reminder every year to compare providers and switch to the best deal going. Only be loyal to your relationships, not your bill providers.
- **Haggle**: a quick phone call to say "I've found a better deal elsewhere" gets you discounts more often than not.
- **Pay annually where you can (like insurance)**: it's often cheaper than monthly instalments (this is where your savings pots will come in handy).
- **Check direct debits**: this is something you should now be doing as part of your money date with yourself. You'd honestly be shocked at how many people are paying for subscriptions they don't even use. The money may as well be going down the drain!

Groceries

- **Meal plan**: this sounds boring, but it saves money and reduces waste.
- **Never shop hungry**: seriously, this tip is underrated. Shopping hungry is dangerous and is proven to make us overspend on things we don't actually need.[7]
- **Swap branded for own brand**: it's often the exact same product in different packaging.
- **Use cashback apps**: like Shopmium or CheckoutSmart for freebies and discounts.

- **Mix fresh and frozen**: frozen fruit and veg are cheaper, last longer, and are just as healthy. This is a hack I've used for years and it saves me a fortune.
- **Try a shop swap**: if you always shop at Tesco, try Aldi or Lidl for a week. See if you notice the difference.

Find your people on the frugal/cheap/savvy spectrum

There are many descriptive words you'll come across within the money community. Three of them that are easily confused are savvy, cheap and frugal – they all differ slightly in their meaning and I think it's handy to know the difference so you can figure out which one applies to you.

- **Frugal**: you're very careful with money, prioritising needs over wants and being very conscious of every money decision. You avoid unnecessary spending and maximise the value of every penny that is spent. You like smart, value-driven spending.
- **Cheap**: you want to spend as little as possible no matter what, sometimes meaning you'll sacrifice quality. Usually being cheap will save you lots of money, but this can come at the cost of something else such as your happiness, convenience and even relationships.
- **Savvy**: you're clever with what you've got, and understand how to work something to the best of your ability. You value getting the most for your money and getting the best deal. It's not always the cheapest option, but it's the most value from the money you have, and it's about spending that money wisely.

Why I love being savvy

I won't insult your intelligence by asking you to guess which camp I'm in.

Personally, I love being savvy. To me, it's about getting the most for your money, being clever with it, and making it work for you. Savvy is my way of living, and not just when it comes to money, because being savvy doesn't just relate to your finances! It's a mindset that can apply to your whole life. It's about being switched on, understanding whatever you're managing and being strategic to get the most from it.

Whichever of these terms best applies to you, own it. There's nothing wrong with any of these approaches (though 'cheap' doesn't *sound* as glam as the others), but by identifying and leaning into your own priorities, you'll be more likely to follow your instincts and make money decisions that bring you peace.

Don't fear being judged

When it comes to money, we often make bad decisions out of fear of being judged by other people. I've been there; I've done it. I've bought another drink when I didn't want to, just to please other people. I've been pressured into buying an add-on in a shop because I don't want them to think I'm being cheap.

I reckon we've all signed up for a charity or service we didn't know anything about and then cancelled the direct debit the next day, only because the shopping-centre sales agent was so persistent.

The same fear can come into play when you first get into saving money. It can manifest in different ways: embarrassment about using a discount code, worrying about saying no to another night out due to your budget, feeling awkward splitting the bill differently because you didn't order as much as everyone else and want to pay only for what you had.

It's easier said than done, but in these moments, remind yourself that judgement says more about the person judging you than it does about you. If you're confident in your money goals, you start to realise that it doesn't matter what anybody else thinks, as long as you're being true to yourself and those goals.

The other day my mum called me 'tight' because I only bought three Lindt balls from the Lindt shop pick n mix. Why is that tight? I got exactly what I wanted! I got to try new flavours, I didn't end up eating 20 sickly chocolate balls I didn't even want, and I stuck to my budget. The only reason this approach gets labelled 'tight' is because there's this weird pressure to fill the bag just because it's there.

The same applies to more than just chocolates.

The earlier you can get over worrying about other people's judgement, the better. Once you stop caring, you'll start saving much more money. It cost me a lot (literally) to learn this lesson, but hopefully I can help you avoid having to learn it the hard way.

Tips to overcome the fear

- **Remember why you're saving**: your goals matter more than strangers' opinions (and if they're not strangers, why are they judging you? What's their issue!)
- **Own your choices**: you know your reasons for why you're doing what you're doing. Own them, and be confident.
- **Flip the script**: someone might call you 'tight' but what does that mean to you? Most of the time it just means you're intentional and savvy with your spending but the person on the other end doesn't have the right money mindset to understand that.
- **Laugh it off**: it's not that deep. Let them have their moment of not understanding your money goals. As long as you understand, that's all that matters. Don't overthink it and let the moment pass.

Chapter tasks

Action one: Choose *one* area of your everyday spending that feels easiest to improve right now. Maybe it's signing up for a cashback site, maybe it's calling your broadband provider to negotiate, or maybe it's doing one meal plan before your next shop. Choose one thing and get it done.

Action two: Have a think and decide whether you're savvy, cheap or frugal.

CHAPTER 3

DEAL WITH YOUR DEBT

DESPITE WHAT YOU might instinctively feel, it's not shameful or embarrassing to talk about debt. In fact, the more we speak about it the less alone people would feel when facing debt. And believe me, if you are in debt, you certainly are *not* alone.

Around 48% of UK adults hold some form of debt, and the average adult UK debt is around £15,000 per household (not including mortgages).[8,9]

Debt statistics always shock me because when we look around we can't *see* debt, we just see the things people buy that gets them *into* debt, which then makes us compare our lifestyle to theirs and feel inadequate because we don't have that stuff. It's one of life's great ironies.

I'm not saying *everybody* who has nice things is now in debt due to them, but it makes you wonder: if almost half the adults in the UK hold some sort of debt, it must be all around us, yet this is what we're comparing ourselves to!

Almost a third of UK adults feel pressure to spend more than they can afford, using credit cards, loans or overdrafts.[10]

Where is this pressure coming from?

Today, it's mainly coming from social media.

The worst thing is, so many people are in it, carrying it around every day, letting it consume them; but nobody really likes to talk about it. It can feel heavy. Lonely. Shameful. It can make you feel like giving up. I know this because I've seen it happen to the people around me. I've seen how hard it is for people to feel all of these things.

The first thing I want to drive home is that *if you are in debt, you're definitely not alone.*

The second is that if you're not in debt, somebody around you may well be.

A lot of people keep their debt hidden. Studies show that around one in six people hide debt from their partner or family, and we know why: because they feel embarrassed and ashamed.

I get it, money is still a taboo subject, we don't like talking about it positively, let alone telling our nearest and dearest that we're in quicksand and our spending has spiralled for whatever reason.

Don't judge when it comes to debt

We live in a society that makes debt easy to fall into. We're constantly surrounded by adverts telling us to treat ourselves, trends on social media designed to lure us into impulse buying, pressure to keep up appearances, and more than ever we're encouraged to spread the cost with endless credit tools instead of paying up front. From Klarna to credit cards to car finance, borrowing has been normalised, yet learning how to manage it hasn't.

Why is this the case? Call me cynical, but it's because when one person *owes* money, someone else is *making* money. The deeper into debt we go, the more money banks and credit providers make from us. Sure, debt is playing its part in making the world go around, but we're on the wrong side of it.

This is why so many people end up stuck. Debt has become part of our everyday lives. It's been normalised. Taking on debt is just how things are done. This is all well and good, until people realise they can't get out of it. And with the cost of living rising, people are depending on credit more than ever.

Debt is a hole that you *can* climb out of with a bit of effort. But it doesn't help that these days the walls are crumbling as quickly as we can climb.

This might sound a little bit emotionally charged, and debt *is* emotional – now let's flip the script, whether you're in this situation yourself or know somebody who's dealing with debt – it's important to know that debt doesn't define a person. Debt is a situation, and just like any situation, it can be changed.

Ignore everyone else's highlight reel

When we see people bringing home the nice cars and fancy clothes, or taking constant days out and sinking round after round of £10 cocktails – how do we know this isn't all being bought on a credit card they can't afford to pay off? In a lot of cases, that's exactly what they're doing. Opening your eyes to this reality is just about the best way to learn that you can't compare yourself to anybody else.

This kind of lifestyle generates a lot of 'bad debt'. You might be thinking *but isn't all debt bad? How can debt be anything* but *bad?*

That's what we've been programmed to think by societal norms and the subconscious money beliefs we developed from a young age. But believe it or not, there is such a thing as good debt.

Recognise that all debt is not created equal

We grow up hearing that we shouldn't get into debt. And it's true, debt really can ruin your life. But I don't think we're ever told that *not all debt is bad debt.* Some debt can actually be good for you. Which might sound shocking if it's the first time you've heard it.

Let's break it down.

Bad debt

This is the type of debt that costs you money and usually gives you absolutely nothing back in return. It's basically paying for something you don't need, with money you don't have, and then paying extra on top (those extortionate interest rates). The most common form of bad debt is consumer debt. This is the debt generated when you use things like Klarna for clothes, credit cards to splurge on meals out that you can't afford, holidays with your friends that get a bit out of hand.

Bad debt is sneaky because at the time it feels harmless. Ever find yourself saying something like, "It's only £30 on Klarna" or "I'll just stick it on the credit card and pay it later"? But the reality is that when you're paying interest, you're losing money every month, and long after that thing you bought (those new trainers, that night out) is gone or the novelty has worn off, the payments are still hanging around – while you have nothing to show for it. People can tend to fall into the trap due to the 'free money windows' such as interest-free credit cards for a certain period of time – which may seem helpful, but can end up building the habit of borrowing.

Someone told me recently that they paid for some garden furniture on credit, and years later they still haven't paid it off. Now they have debt collectors chasing the payment. They said they don't want to pay for it now because they bought it years ago and don't even like the furniture anymore. Today's money is paying for a decade-old impulse spend. It's humiliating, and I think this sums up how debt makes a lot of people feel.

They don't have anything to show for the money they've spent, just a lingering sense of shame at their own mistakes and a hungry pit where their money goes to die.

Good debt

Now, let's talk about the side of debt nobody really shouts about.

Good debt is debt that works for *you*.

It's when borrowing money helps you make more money, or essentially builds you a better financial future. Good debt either:

1. Helps you grow your wealth.
2. Improves your life long-term in a way that makes sense financially.

Examples of good debt include:

- **A mortgage**: probably the biggest debt any of us will have in our lifetime. It's a huge debt, but it's tied to an asset (your home) that usually grows in value over time.
- **Student loans**: they can feel like a burden, but education usually increases your earning potential for life if you do something with your degree or qualification.
- **Investing in a business**: taking a loan to start or grow a business can be good if it eventually leads to bringing in more income.

For years we've all been fed the idea that *all* debt is bad. We hear that borrowing is risky; don't borrow too much or else you'll damage your credit score; don't get into debt full-stop; don't touch credit cards. A lot of this is true when you don't have systems in place, and also if you're not provided with the right tools to utilise debt properly. Like everything, it's the way we use it, and the way we're taught (or not taught) to manage it.

And don't forget that a good workman never blames his tools.

I'm sharing everything with you in this book, and the truth is that I've never been in bad debt. This isn't a "look at me!" moment, and it's certainly not because I'm some money genius who's had it all figured out since day one. If anything, it's quite the opposite. I think my upbringing traumatised me into hoarding money and never risking anything, especially not someone else's money. I guess that trauma was lucky for me, because it meant I didn't fall into a debt cycle. It's the silver lining to a troubled start with money, but many people didn't benefit from this type of early aversion to debt.

The sad truth is that most of us weren't taught *anything* about money growing up. We weren't shown how credit cards really work, how interest adds up or even how to know what interest rate we're paying and how much that can really make debt spiral. So many people end up in bad debt not because they're careless, but because they were never given the tools to avoid it in the first place.

If you are in debt right now, it's never too late to flip the script. There's always a light at the end of the tunnel. I've seen so many people's debt journeys turn around, even when they didn't believe that it would ever happen for them.

Before we get into how you can do that too, here's a little bit of the credit card lingo (but it applies to most forms of debt) it's important to understand when figuring your way out of debt:

- **Billing cycle**: the period your credit card company tracks your spending for (usually 30 days). At the end of it, they send you a statement of what you owe. Pay it in full by the due date and you won't pay interest. Make sure you're familiar with the billing cycle of any credit cards you own, and try to pay off all spending before the due date if you can.
- **APR (annual percentage rate)**: this is how much the credit card company charges you in interest if you don't pay your balance in full. It's shown as a yearly percentage, but really it's the cost of borrowing. When taking on any debt, make sure you're choosing an option with a competitively low APR.

- **Interest-free period**: most credit cards give you around 50–56 days interest free if you clear the balance in full. If you don't, that's when the interest kicks in. Make sure you take advantage of this window of opportunity; it's the closest credit cards come to offering free money (but remember it's not free, it's just the only way that repayment won't cost more than the amount you borrow).
- **Minimum payment**: the absolute lowest amount you can pay each month. This might seem a small amount, but paying the minimum keeps you in debt for longer because the interest will rack up. Still, paying the minimum is much better than failing to pay even that. Minimum payments on all debt need to be your top priority.
- **Balance transfer**: moving your debt from one card (with interest) to another card with a 0% interest offer, usually for something like six to nine months. This can give you a breather and help you pay off your balance quicker without having to pay interest on top. You'll usually pay a flat fee for the transfer, but this will tend to be less than the interest you would have racked up on your old card.
- **Credit limit**: the maximum amount you're allowed to spend on the card at any one time. It might be tempting to go for a card with a huge limit, but that introduces the temptation to spend up to that limit. The less you borrow, the less you'll have to pay back.
- **Consumer Credit Act protection (Section 75)**: this is a gem. If you buy something between £100 and £30,000 on your credit card and it goes wrong (the company goes bust, item never arrives, item is faulty, etc.), your card provider has to protect you. It's a good reason to buy big purchases on a credit card as long as you can pay them off.

Ways to pay off your debt faster

I don't want you to just understand debt better, I want you to have practical tips and methods to help pay off your debt.

Let's take a look at how to pay off debt *faster*, because the quicker you can take control of debt, the quicker you can move towards financial control and even financial freedom.

There are two very common methods that will help you get a hold of your debt and tackle it head on.

1. The snowball method

This method is all about the momentum of your money. You start by paying off your smallest debt first, while keeping up the minimum payments on everything else. Once that smallest one is gone, you move to the next smallest, and so on.

Why it works: you get quick wins. Each time you cross off a debt, you feel amazing. That motivation pushes you to keep going.

Start by:

- **Listing all of your debts**: total balance, minimum payment, interest rates.
- **Order them by value**: from smallest debt to highest debt.
- **Make those minimum payments**: on all debts apart from the smallest debt. The smallest debt gets your full attention with every spare pound you can find.
- **Fire away with any extra money**: from a side hustle, selling your old stuff, a bonus; throw it all at that smallest-value debt to get it paid off.
- **Repeat the process**: once that smallest debt is paid off, you can then start throwing the same amount at the next-smallest debt re-payment.

2. The avalanche method

This is the more maths-oriented method. Instead of going for the smallest debt, you go for the one with the *highest interest rate* first. Once that's gone, you tackle the next highest, and so on.

Why it works: you'll pay less in interest overall, which means you get debt-free quicker and save yourself money in the process. It may not feel as fast as the snowball method, but it's a great way to pay off your debt.

Start by:

- **Listing all of your debts**: total balance, minimum payment, interest rates.
- **Order them by interest rates**: highest to lowest.
- **Make those minimum payments**: on all debts apart from the one with the highest interest. The highest-interest debt gets your full attention with every spare pound you can find.
- **Fire away with any extra money**: from a side hustle, selling your old stuff, a bonus; throw it all at that high-interest debt to get it paid off.
- **Repeat the process**: once that highest-interest debt is paid off (yes that day will come!) you can then start throwing the same amount at the next-highest-interest debt payment.

I've watched family members, friends and even social media people that I follow go through inspiring debt journeys, and while I haven't been in that debt cycle myself, I've learned a lot about debt from seeing people that mean a lot to me go through it.

Once you've found a method, consistency is key. It's going to feel hard; you're probably going to feel like you're fighting a losing battle at some points (but you're not, slow progress is still progress). Stick to the steps, focus on the bigger picture, and don't forget to celebrate those milestones, no matter how small!

I'm not going to stop there, because there's more you can do to tackle debt than just following one of these methods. I also have some every-day, practical steps to help you and to keep you motivated on your debt-tackling journey.

1. **Extra money? Throw it at the debt**: when it comes to debt, and specifically interest rates, every little helps. Throw any extra money you have at the debt. Don't take this *too* literally. You don't need to bleed yourself dry and live on beans on toast until you become debt-free – but if there's any surprising money that pops up, you take on a side hustle or you go on a declutter spree and earn some extra cash – throw it at that debt.
2. **Automation is your bestie**: let's be realistic, sometimes motivation and willpower are not enough to get you through. Just like the gym, it's in the consistency that we see results. Set up payments or direct debits to do the hard work for you.
3. **Helpful financial tools**: you can look into moving high-interest debt to a 0% balance transfer card or consolidating into a lower-interest loan. You can also look into affordability complaints, or even simply asking the bank if they can lower your interest rate. One of my life mottos is 'you don't ask, you don't get' – what's the worst they can say?
4. **Track that progress**: we've already got enough going on in our brains, we cannot mentally track every detail of our debt progress. Write it down, get a lovely chart going, something visually pleasing. Something that gives you the motivation to keep going on your down days.

Helpful resources and helplines

If you are in the UK and you or someone you know needs some help, guidance or support when it comes to debt, here are a few places you can reach out to:

- **Step Change**: a charity that offers free debt support and advice: stepchange.org.uk.
- **National Debtline (England and Wales)**: a trusted debt advice charity: nationaldebtline.org.
- **Citizens Advice**: advice centres and website that offer independent advice: www.citizensadvice.org.uk.
- **Community Money Advice**: centres to help with debt advice: www.communitymoneyadvice.com.

Debt is one huge part of the financial landscape, but it's one where it's easy to get lost in the gory details. Next we're going to pull back our perspective a little to take a look at the wider financial landscape – the picture of our financial health and the impact it can have on our relationships.

Chapter tasks

Action: If you're in debt, pick the repayment method that sounds best to you and implement it. Use the actionable tips we've covered here to help you stay on track.

If you're not struggling with debt, your good deed for the day is to help someone you who is (or who you think might be) - whether it's talking through their options or maybe even lending this book to them. That's an act of kindness in itself!

CHAPTER 4

GET FINANCIALLY FIT IN YOUR HEALTH AND RELATIONSHIPS

I HOPE BY THIS point you're feeling confident and raring to go with getting your finances in order, establishing a budget and working on your mindful spending. After we've taken these first steps on our money journey, the next stage is something we *all* have to do: look after our financial health and relationships.

Maintaining your financial health

It's one thing to make changes, but we all know it's another to keep them going. Just like the healthiness of any other area of our life, whether fitness, mental wellbeing or diet, it's not about doing one big thing once – it's about the consistency. It's about building habits, staying the course and checking in with yourself so you can keep moving in the right direction. It can also be about changing things if they're not heading in that direction.

Here's why checking in matters:

- **Life changes**: jobs change, bills go up, kids (or fur babies) come along, relationships break down, emergencies happen. What worked last year might not work this year.
- **Habits can slip**: if you take your eye off the ball, it's easy to fall back into old spending patterns without even realising it.
- **Goalposts move**: what you wanted at 25 isn't the same as what you want at 35. Your goals *will* change.

If you're not regularly checking in on your money, you can't make the changes you need to make room for any of the above. Keeping an eye on things and adjusting as you go – and as life changes – is how you stay in control.

Check in on your finances

If there's *one thing* you take from this book (though obviously I'd love for you to take it all, please) it's that setting up a regular money date with yourself is a must. We have already set these up for you in your tasks for Chapter 1, but as your finances begin to stabilise we can move from 'foundational money dates' to 'maintenance money dates'. These still don't need to be boring or stressful. Put on some music, grab a coffee (or wine), light a candle, and spend an hour looking over your money.

Ask yourself:

- Am I sticking to my budget?
- Have my expenses gone up or down this month?
- Am I making progress towards my savings goals?
- Do I need to adjust anything for next month?

Without checking in, it's all just guesswork, and we can't afford to guess when it comes to money. Knowing where you stand is key to staying in control and a money date is exactly how to do that.

Change your money plan with the times

Your financial plan is not set in stone.

It's supposed to be flexible. Too many people feel like once they make a budget, they're locked into it, but how boring would that be? Besides, that's just not how it works – because things change. Life changes constantly. You might get a pay rise (wahoo!), or you might have a relationship break down (boo!). You might welcome a new baby or decide to move house. Whatever it is, your budget and your goals need to move with your life.

Don't be afraid to tweak things. The same plan won't work forever. Sometimes change can be a scary thing, especially when it comes to our money, but we'd much rather plan ahead for changes than get stuck in the middle of them and see our money bear the brunt of it.

Find your balance

A lot of people think managing money is about cutting back, saying no, and saving every last penny. This assumption pains me because it couldn't be further from the truth! You can't be all of one and none of the other. Money isn't just for spending, it's for saving too – just like it's not just for saving, it's for spending too! Life is for living; money is there to enjoy. We work hard enough for it, and managing your money is not supposed to take all of that away.

If you're spending all of your money and not saving any, you're going to struggle in the future, but if you're saving everything and never spending on yourself, you're not living. That's scarcity, and it's not healthy! Trust me, having been there, I know that it's not a nice place to be.

A balanced approach looks like this:

- Saving for your future while enjoying the current moment.
- Saying no to things that don't serve you, so you can say yes to things that do.
- Avoiding lifestyle creep (when your spending rises every time your income does), but still upgrading your life in ways that actually matter to you.
- Understanding that money is a tool to use in a way that will benefit you.

Celebrate your wins

We're so focused on the next step, the next goal, the next amount to save, that we forget to stop and celebrate how far we've already come.

Celebrating along the way matters – I don't think any of us celebrate enough of our own milestones and wins.

If you've saved £100 when before you saved nothing, celebrate that. If you've stuck to your budget for a whole month, celebrate that. If you paid off one credit card, celebrate that. These are all huge wins, even if they feel small to you at the time.

You might find this awkward at first, but you don't need to go over the top to celebrate (but by all means throw a party every time you pass on a coffee shop latte if that's you!). Your celebration could be something as simple as telling a friend, sharing your wins online, treating yourself to something. It doesn't matter how the celebration looks; the point is that you're recognising your own effort.

Studies show that celebrating small wins increases motivation, builds confidence, and makes you more likely to stick to your goals for the long term. The more you acknowledge your progress, the more progress you'll make.[11]

Bring it all together

It's time to bring it all together! No matter where you're starting, maintaining your financial health is something we all need to do. Whether you're paying off debt, saving your first £500 or investing for your future – it's all maintained the same:

- Check in on your money regularly.
- Adjust as life changes.
- Keep your approach balanced.
- Celebrate your wins along the way.

When you do these things, money becomes less of a stress and more of a tool to support your life, which is exactly what it's meant to be for everybody!

Make money a healthy part of healthy relationships

There's no way to sugar coat this: money and relationships can cause each other problems. Romance and relationships are actually a significant reason behind many people getting into debt. According to a data study from Experian, 5% of young men have got themselves into over £10,000 of debt from dating or relationships. I don't even find that hard to believe.

Truth is, money is not something a person really thinks about when they first start dating a new partner. Love is in the air, their heart is constantly fluttering, and they get weak at the knees when their new person enters the room. How are they supposed to step back and estimate how much money this relationship is going to cost them now and in the long run? Not very romantic, is it?

Financial incompatibility can be a dealbreaker

We check for chemistry, we check for attraction, we check for shared hobbies – but do we ever check a new partner for financial compatibility? Not often enough, because money is one of the leading causes of arguments and breakups in relationships.

Being on the same page financially means you understand each other's values and goals when it comes to money. Are they a spender or a saver? Are they a YOLO type of person or do they plan their future?

The earlier you find these things out, the better. Some people say this is shallow, but actually it's almost the opposite, it's very sensible! You don't have to sit across from someone on a first date and demand their credit score (please *don't* do that), but you *can* weave money questions into natural conversations:

"How do you feel about splitting the bill?"

"Would you say you're more of a saver or a spender?"

"If you had £1,000 extra right now, what would you do with it?"

It's a way to gauge their money mindset without directly intruding on their finances (because although money shouldn't be a taboo subject, it currently still is, and we definitely want to ease ourselves in on a first date).

Why it's good to find out early

Just like any type of compatibility, financial compatibility is an important one to figure out as early as possible to avoid any issues in the long run. Do you want to be with a partner who hides things from you when it comes to money or can drag you down into debt (flashback to my mum's mistakes here)?

Sometimes the incompatibility isn't as serious as these scenarios, but it's important to know about the little things too: what sort of dates they can realistically afford to go on, if they have expensive taste or like things simple and budget-friendly, or even if they're reliable enough with money to split bills if and when you move in together.

I remember when my partner and I went on our third date together. During dinner he asked me whether I saved money and if I thought it was important. I remember being surprised (in a good way) that money had come up so early. It told me a lot about him and his attitude towards money, and it told me at an early enough stage in our relationship that I could make meaningful choices based on that knowledge. He wasn't afraid to talk about money, which was refreshing.

Let's be honest, we probably all wish we could just ask those money questions outright, because deep down we all want to know how much our date earns (or is that just me?).

I insisted on paying for that dinner, after he'd covered the previous few, because I didn't want there to be this assumption that he had to take on all the financial responsibility. It didn't feel like a huge deal at the time, but that conversation, and that small gesture from me really did set the tone for how open we'd be about money.

Many people don't ask questions like these in the early days, because money still feels like a taboo subject. We ask about hobbies, their family, their friends, so why not weave money in there too? It'll definitely set a future relationship up on a strong financial foundation.

Don't be tempted to commit financial infidelity

When I was a guest on Experian's podcast *The Cost of Loving with Anna Williamson*, we had a huge discussion about something many couples face: financial infidelity. That's when couples hide money from each other, whether it's secret debt, hidden savings or downplaying how much they earn.

This phenomenon is more common than you might think.

According to a survey by Finder, 39% of UK adults admit to committing financial infidelity in relationships, but would this statistic be as high if people actually addressed their financial compatibility before getting serious?

Finance is one thing I truly believe should be an open book when it comes to your romantic partner, not in the sense that you have to share your finances and have a joint account and live in each other's pockets, watching every time one another spends, but more that nothing should ever be kept a secret. Money and partners seem to be a common theme of secrecy on social media – usually at the expense of the husband (see those generational gender roles coming into play again?).

I see videos constantly of women saying they're hiding their parcels from their husband, asking the postman to throw them over the back gate so their partner doesn't see, their partner's reaction when they find out they've spent £100+ on skincare – these jokes go on and on.

Sometimes these *are* just jokes, and they're light-hearted. I don't want to be the Negative Nelly, but the problem is that when you look deeply into these trends, they're continuing the narrative that women can't be good with money, and that men are in control of the finances.

Another problem with these jokes is that they make secrecy in relationships feel normal and something to laugh about. But if we're laughing about hiding shopping bags, where do we draw the line?

If we really want to change the narrative around money, especially for women, we have to stop treating secrecy as normal. There should be no shame or sneaking when it comes to how you handle your money, and if there *is* shame or sneaking, there is more than likely an underlying spending issue.

Being an open book builds trust when it comes to money. So be open and confident by saying "This is me, this is how I spend, this is how I save." When both partners are upfront, it creates a safe space for honest conversations instead of feeling like you need to hide things or be secretive.

Money doesn't have to be a sore subject or create a feeling of awkwardness. It can actually be a way to build together, but that can only happen if both people are honest and open.

The sooner we ditch the secrecy and not-so-funny money jokes, the sooner we can change the narrative and create healthier, happier money conversations in our relationships.

How to stay open about money in a relationship:

- **Talk about money early**: it doesn't need to be heavy, just weave it into normal conversation.
- **Be honest about spending habits**: own your habits. If you're a spender, say so. If you're a saver, let them know.
- **Set boundaries together**: if you're getting serious with each other (or already are), agree on boundaries. What should you chat about when it comes to spending money? What's personal to each of you, and what needs to be a mutual decision?
- **No secrets**: let's be real, there should be no secrets when it comes to money in a relationship. Hiding debt, purchases, savings or income will just create a divide and eat away at trust.

Budget and set goals as a couple

If you're in a relationship, your money goals need to align. Otherwise, you'll always feel like you're pulling in opposite directions and arguing over money.

Invite your partner to your regular money dates to look at bills but also to talk about the bigger picture, your individual goals and goals you want to reach together.

Split bills in a way that feels fair. This could be 50/50 or proportional to income. There's no right or wrong way, as long as it works for both of you, but resentment builds when one partner feels they're carrying more weight.

Make sure you agree about fun money. You both deserve to enjoy your money, but it should feel fair, and nobody should feel they have to hide anything. Map it out together, and there'll never be any second guessing.

Money and friendships

It's not just with romantic partners that money matters. Friendships can be tested by money too. I've lost friends when I learned to say no to things that don't serve me.

How many times have you been called boring for saying no? For skipping a night out because money is tight? Or for not wanting to split a bill evenly when you didn't even touch the cocktails? (This last one has happened to me too many times because I'm not a drinker, but no, I do not want to split the bill and pay for your £10 cocktails!)

Friendship should never be conditional on spending money you don't have, but because money talk feels awkward, we often say yes when we should say no, and then resent it later.

The message here isn't to ditch your friends if your money goals don't align, because of course everyone's different, but you can definitely start having more honest conversations, just like you would with a romantic partner.

Here are some of the common pitfalls when it comes to friends and money.

Comparison

The comparison trap is easy to fall into, especially with the people closest to you. The fact is, it does show up a lot in friendships.

I've had friends who always seem to be out, buying new clothes every week or upgrading their lifestyle constantly. I'd be lying if I said I've never thought that I should be doing that too, but over the years I've learned that their choices are their own, just like your choice is yours. The two don't have to match.

We all have different goals, different financial situations, different money mindsets – there is no right or wrong path to be on.

When you catch yourself comparing, it's worth reminding yourself:

- You don't know the full picture of someone else's finances (credit card debt doesn't show on Instagram).
- You've got your own financial goals that will look different.
- Someone else's spending habits aren't a reflection of what you should be doing with your money.

The jealousy factor

Comparison and jealousy are similar, but subtly different. More often than not, when jealousy creeps into friendships, money is at least a part of the cause (if sometimes indirectly).

Whether it's about what someone else has, what they're buying or what they're doing, it's money at the root of it.

Jealousy might not come from you; it might be you on the receiving end. If you're smashing your goals, building your career, going the 'right' way in life and towards your goals, you might feel the green-eyed monster staring at you. You can't always put your finger on why someone's acting a certain way towards you, why the energy has shifted. We sometimes think it's jealousy but don't want to toot our own horn or put someone else down. Even so, it's important to spot the signs early on, and don't be tempted to think that you're the issue. If someone's jealous of your financial situation, the problem comes from their own relationship with money.

If jealousy (on either side) starts to take over, it can be better to let the friendship fizzle out naturally than to let resentment take over. Remember that this isn't a deep romance. It doesn't need to be a dramatic breakup. Sometimes it's just about stepping back, acknowledging the problem and protecting your own peace.

I've had to do this a few times throughout my life. Growing up in an environment where money is scarce, where people are living to work, when you start to go against the grain, and away from the 'norm', people can start to feel differently towards you. In my younger years, I used to think *what's wrong with me? Maybe I'm the problem*, but as I learned more about money and money mindset, I realised, there's nothing wrong with me, I'm just at a different stage of my life, and have a different mindset to the people around me, and I just haven't found my circle of 'people' yet.

How to say no, without actually saying no

Rewinding to the time before I learnt that it's okay to let friendships go, I experienced so many times where I've wanted to say no while not wanting to say no, due to people-pleasing, not wanting to upset anybody or not wanting to look 'tight'.

I know this is something a lot of people struggle with, to say no – so I'm sharing my ways to say no without actually saying no:

- I'm not feeling going out-out but why don't you come round to mine for a catch-up?
- I'm on a saving journey at the moment. I'd still love to meet up though, shall we go for a walk?
- That won't work for me, you can go ahead without me and I'll see if I can join next time.
- Shall I pop over to yours instead of going out? I'm trying not to spend much at the moment.

Being open and honest is all you can do. These suggestions are all polite and considerate while putting yourself first. If anybody has a problem with that, that's definitely a 'them' issue!

Similarly, if friends can't respect your values and goals when it comes to money, that definitely says more about them than it does about you. Finances can get tricky in friendship groups, because everybody is so different, and naturally we do judge what others choose to spend their money on, especially if it's something that we totally would not spend our money on. But the more we talk about money, discuss money goals, habits or even worries, the more accepting and considerate of other people's situations we become – which is a win-win for everybody isn't it!?

Talking about money might feel awkward at first, but the more you do it, the easier it becomes. When we normalise money talk with the people closest to us, it causes a ripple effect. It stops being taboo. It builds confidence, and people take this and let it compound, and before you know it, money will become less of a taboo subject.

CHAPTER 5

FUTURE YOU: SAVING FOR YOUR GOALS

YOU'VE NOW HAD a chance to think about your *why*, and this is something we'll revisit when looking to the future. Firstly, it's the thing that makes everybody's financial journeys so different. Everybody's 'why' will be unique, which will make their financial journey unique and personal.

Your 'why' will play a huge part in setting your money goals, and figuring out what your goals actually are. We want to know what's important to you, not what anybody else thinks is important, not what you feel influenced to think is important, what you truly think is important.

For this reason, when defining your why it's important to reflect and make sure you're not acting as a content sponge: someone who soaks in everything they hear on social media without realising what they actually believe to be right or wrong, true or false, a load of bull or actually useful. This trap is easier to fall into than you might think.

We're marketed to 24/7, we hear other people's thoughts and opinions through social media constantly, and it's hard not to be what I call a 'content sponge'.

My definition of a content sponge: someone who soaks in everything they hear on social media without realising what they actually believe to be right or wrong, true or false, a load of bull or actually useful.

If you're thinking *sh**, I think I'm a content sponge!* that's actually okay! Most of us (including me) either are or have been through the stage of being one, it's only natural when most of our spare time is taken up by social media. That's why I'm focusing on this, to make you aware of your own opinions, things that are truly important to you, your 'why'.

Once you're confident you've figured out your 'why', and what's really important to you, you can start to pave out the way to your money goals and what you're trying to achieve.

Know what you mean when you say you want to be rich

I've come to the educated assumption that most people who haven't yet embarked on their money journey think that one day, in the future, they'll be rich, that they'll have enough money to live out their dreams. They don't know how, they just have this picture in their head that they'll get there one day.

I'll tell you how I made this assumption… It's because I had this vision before I started taking my own money journey seriously. I just envisioned future me, in my head, in a big house, lots of money, a nice car with the dreamy dream that one day I'll have lots of money and it'll all be lovely. I didn't have a clue how I'd get there, but I just ignorantly thought I'd get there because I have lots of time to get there. My partner also has a similar vision – and I'm sure you've heard multiple people in your lifetime begin a sentence with "When I'm rich…" or "One day, when I'm wealthy…" Often these are only pipedreams, because there's no real plan, no goals in place, no route to achieving these things. After all, without a route, how can you get anywhere?

Nothing changes if nothing changes. Life isn't going to miraculously make you rich. Time ticks on, and it passes whether you do anything with it or not. We're never going to get rich if we don't establish the route to getting there.

In case you're wondering, I should tell you that manifestation and a dreamy dream are not enough to get you there either. I learned that the hard way!

But when we say we want to be rich, what do we even mean? What is rich? Rich isn't just a monetary figure. It's a whole load of things. Let me tell you what rich means to me, and I want you to have a think about what rich really means to you.

Rich to me is being rich not only in money, but in health, in family, in memories, in experiences. There's being financially rich, and then there's having a *rich life*.

What rich means to you should coincide with what 'money' means to you (and hopefully you wrote that down when I told you to!).

You should now have these three things:

1. What money means to you.
2. Your *why*.
3. Your own definition of rich.

Now you've got the foundation to set out some goals!

The love of money

If your version of 'rich' really is just about the money, heck yeah, good for you. I've said it before and I'll say it again – it is not shallow to want more money, it's not shallow to love money. We should all love it!

There are people out there with absolutely sh**loads of it, and deep down I bet almost everybody who isn't monetarily super rich wishes that was them. The heavens above know I wish I was a billionaire! (A few million would actually be fine but hey, why not aim high!?) Why does it feel almost shameful to admit we love money? Society. That's why.

You've read enough by now to know that money is pivotal to have options in life, to create freedom, and most importantly that money isn't good nor bad, it's what we do with it that makes the difference. Don't let society have you believing that you shouldn't want to *want* more money!

Money doesn't buy happiness... or does it?

I'm sure you've heard people say "Money doesn't buy happiness." I know I have, probably more times than I can count. I don't actually think it's a phrase people say because they truly believe it. I think, deep down, it's often something we tell ourselves when money feels tight, to make us feel better about not having as much as we'd like. And please don't get this twisted, this isn't me being condescending because here's the truth: I'm not here to debate whether money can buy happiness or not, because happiness means different things to different people. What I *am* here to say is this: it's not shallow to want more money. Wanting more money doesn't make you greedy. I might sound like a broken record, but I cannot stress this enough!

Money is a tool. It buys options. It can reduce stress, open doors and free up time to spend with your family, to travel, to work less, to pursue passions. It might not directly buy happiness but it can absolutely create an environment where happiness has more room to grow.

Let's be real, so many of our stresses are linked to money. Studies show that money is the biggest cause of arguments in UK households;[12] a survey showed that almost 90% of Brits say money worries impact their sleep at night;[13] and debt charity StepChange reported that money issues are linked to mental health problems in almost half of their clients.[14]

If money worries cause stress, tension and even breakdowns in relationships, then surely having *less* of that stress through financial security would create *more* space for happiness?

Think about it:

- Having enough money means you don't have to argue over bills with your partner.
- It means you can afford proper healthcare without waiting months on a list (we're so grateful for the NHS in the UK, but waitlist times would be nice not to deal with).
- It means freedom, whether that's retiring earlier, working fewer hours or simply not living paycheck to paycheck.
- You can go to bed at night without that money worry.

I think we can agree that money can create a less stressful, more secure, more enjoyable life where we can all thrive, and that for me is worth wanting. Any one of them could be a worthy goal. Whether your goals look like this or are completely different, you'll need to set some checkpoints along the way.

Short- and long-term goals

Some of your money goals will be short term, and as much as we'd probably like to reach all of our money goals in the short term, we'll have long-term goals too. Short term can be anything from a couple of months to a couple of years. This can be things like:

- Saving up for your next holiday.
- Paying off a small credit card debt.
- Starting to build up your emergency fund.

These short-term goals are like quick wins. They keep you motivated, they give you something to celebrate and be proud of and they give you that dopamine hit you need.

Then you've got your long-term goals. These are the *big* ones.

Long-term goals might include:

- Buying a house.
- Setting up a retirement fund.
- Building generational wealth for your kids.

Whatever your long-term goals are, they can take years, sometimes even decades to achieve, but they're the reason you're learning to manage your money in the first place, right now.

Here's the important thing, though: short- and long-term goals aren't in separate lanes. They actually intertwine. Paying off debt (short term) frees up more money to invest for the future (long term). Building an emergency fund (short term) gives you stability so you can take bigger risks later (long term). Even something as simple as cutting back on takeaways for a few months might give you the savings to book that family holiday or even something like starting to invest consistently each month into a stocks and shares ISA.

And it's not just money goals either. Think about your non-money goals, things like wanting to feel healthier, less stressed, spend more time with your kids, family… They're linked to your finances. Getting your money sorted reduces stress. Being able to afford a gym membership or meal-prep can support your health and give you more time. Making your money work for you gives you that extra time with your family.

Money doesn't sit in a box on its own, it's woven into every part of your life, and as I've said before, it really does make the world go around.

Achieving those goals

It's 1st January, and you've set those new year's resolutions… 31st March comes around and you've forgotten all about them, heck you may not even remember what those resolutions were. I'm guiltyyyyy. I've done this, have you?

Don't let this happen to your goals. This only happens because you've set a goal, but no path to get there. You've got the end destination, but where's the journey?

The 'getting there' bit is where most people fall off, and that's for one of two reasons, overcomplicating it, or not planning at all. It doesn't need to be fancy, complicated, it just needs to be practical, clear and doable.

Rewind

It actually helps to work your way backwards. Look at your goal, and break it down into bite-sized pieces. Want £1,200 saved for Christmas in 12 months? That's £100 a month. Want £10,000 for a house deposit in five years? That's £2,000 a year, or around £167 a month. Breaking it down like this takes away the scariness. It breaks a big goal into small, manageable chunks, and small steps are way more achievable.

Once you know your number, decide where that money's coming from. Is it cutting your budget, getting rid of a monthly takeaway you don't really need, cancelling a subscription you don't use? Or maybe it's a side hustle… Or even simply becoming a tad smarter on the money you're already spending by using cashback, discounts and freebies!

Automate it

We've touched on automation before, but it really is such a lifesaver that I want to reiterate its importance here. You've made the plan to achieve your goals, now make it easier for yourself, because we know that sometimes willpower just doesn't cut it.

You need to think of your savings like a bill, a bill you have no choice but to pay. You wouldn't skip paying your rent, your mortgage, an energy bill, so why skip paying yourself? You are in control, make it a priority.

Set up a standing order or direct debit so that as soon as you get paid, money automatically moves into your savings pot, before you even see it sitting in your account. Out of sight, out of mind, but really it's stacking up towards your goal in the background.

By making it automatic, you take the temptation and mundane process out of it. You don't have to 'try' and save because it's just doing it for you.

Look into the FIRE

Have you heard of the FIRE movement?

FIRE stands for Financial Independence, Retire Early. It's all about saving and investing as aggressively as possible so financial independence and freedom can be reached way earlier than the typical retirement age.

Why do people do it? Because many of us don't want to spend 40+ years working a job we don't love just to scrape by when we're old. FIRE is about buying back your time and your freedom while you're still young enough to enjoy it.

FIRE principles:

- **Live below your means**: cutting expenses drastically to save a high percentage of your income.
- **Increase income**: side hustles, career growth, investing.
- **Invest early and often**: instead of leaving money in savings, you rely on compound growth through your investment.
- **Getting your number**: work out how much you need invested to cover your living costs for life.

So why am I telling you this?

I'm not telling you to have FIRE as your goal, and you don't have to use the FIRE label or join any kind of community. For example, one of my goals is to reach retirement as early as possible, but I don't label myself within the FIRE movement, though we can take a lot from the mindset behind the FIRE movement.

It makes you think differently about money.

It challenges the idea that we *have* to work until our 60s.

It shows that intentional saving and investing can buy you freedom and choices, whether that's retiring early, going part-time, starting a business or even just feeling less stressed about money.

For some, FIRE means retiring at 40. For others, it could just mean being able to go part-time at 50, or having the freedom to change careers without money being an issue.

It's creating choices, and that's what our money should be about.

Creative ways to save more money

Sometimes you can cut back as much as possible and it still feels like there's nothing left. If you feel like you're in that position but have all these huge goals, how do you *really* save more money?

There's only so much cutting back you can do.

I've been heavy on the "life is for living" and "it's all about balance" and it doesn't stop here just because we've got goals to reach. Yes, I'm a firm believer that sacrifice is necessary to achieve what we want to achieve, but it really doesn't have to be doom and gloom and getting rid of the joy in everything, because there's always sneaky and clever little ways to build up your savings pot without feeling like you're sacrificing the things you love.

1. Round-up apps (aka saving without noticing)

These are one of my favourite hacks because you literally don't feel it happening. Round-up apps work by rounding your spending to the nearest pound and saving the difference. Spend £2.40 on a morning coffee – 60p goes into your savings. It's small, but those little pennies add up without you even trying. Before you know it, you've got a little pot building up. Lots of banks offer this feature now, but there's also specialist apps that connect to your spending card that can do it for you.

2. Saving challenges

Here they are again! You've probably seen the viral '1p challenge' in which you start by saving 1p on day one, 2p on day two and so on. By the end of the year, you've saved over £600. It doesn't have to be this exact challenge, but something that makes it fun for you. Try a 'no spend day' challenge, where you aim for one or two days a week where you spend nothing. Or a 'side hustle challenge' where you set a goal to side hustle X amount every month.

3. Sell your junk

This is the most underrated way to make money, fast. One man's trash is another man's treasure, and in the glorious age we're in of re-selling apps and sites, it's never been easier. We've all got that cupboard, wardrobe or drawer full of stuff we never use! Clothes, tech, toys, furniture. It's a double, triple whammy because not only are you putting money into your own pocket, you're being economically friendly and decluttering your space too.

4. Side hustle your way there

This isn't about quitting your job or burning yourself out by doing too much, but by now it's probably clear that I love a side hustle. If you can't cut back from what's already coming in, we simply need to make more money, and we'll get into this soon, but you really can make money from anything! Even an extra £50 a month adds up to £600 a year!

5. Cashback and discounts

Remember how I said earlier that cashback is one of my favourite things ever? It's because you can literally save money as you spend money. It's just genius. You can direct every penny of cashback straight into your savings.

The thing is, with cutting back, there's a limit, but when you get creative, the limit does not exist (*Mean Girls* fans, where you at?).

You can get as creative as you want to make more money and to make the money you already have stretch further. People don't suddenly save thousands by living off beans on toast for years, and we don't want that, do we? We want to enjoy the process – being intentional, setting clear goals, with a clear pathway, getting creative and focusing on the small wins that turn into big achievements over time.

You're now starting to be savvier with your money, and saving even more from these little habits, so how can we start to make this money work for you over the long term (other than investing, which gets a chapter all to itself)?

Plan for later life

Most of us don't like thinking about old age, but while we're on the subject of future you, I had to drop it in here, even if it's just food for thought. I don't like thinking about being old, but it is important to think about it, especially when it comes to your retirement. I know it feels like it's ages away and you'd like to think you can deal with it when the time comes… but when it comes to your pension, you *have* to think early! Whether you're in your 20s, 30s, 40s or even 50s, the choices you make now will directly shape what life looks like when you stop working.

Fail to plan, plan to fail. Failing to plan isn't something you want to be regretting as you come closer to drawing your pension.

You work so hard for your money, we all do, and you really don't want that to carry into old age; that's the time when we've paid our dues, and it's the time to sit back and actually enjoy our time and money… and your decisions right now are in control of that. Why not make sure that future you isn't stressed about bills, or having to work longer than you'd like?

The State Pension – it's just not enough

Let me start by saying, we're lucky to have a state pension in the UK, I'm not knocking that privilege, but it's definitely not there to give you a lovely comfortable retirement, it's purely there to help you survive. Who wants to be just getting by and 'surviving' in their older age?

This is the time a lot of us dream about – how many times have you heard people say 'Can I retire now?' 'I can't wait to retire!' Yet some of these people haven't even thought about their pensions, and they'll definitely have a shock relying on just State Pension (and who knows what it'll actually look like by the time we get there, or if it will even still exist!?).

The State Pension in 2024/25 is £221.20 per week, about £11,502 a year. For so many people that won't even cover the basics, let alone factoring in any fun hobbies or holidays.

The state pension age keeps rising. It's currently 66, moving to 67 by 2028, and may go even higher in future. If that happens, you'll be waiting longer to access it, which means you'll be working even longer (that's if you don't plan for your own retirement).

Building your own retirement plan isn't even a luxury anymore; I'd say it's more a necessity.

Creating your own pension pot

Having your own pension means you're not relying on the state alone. I definitely don't want to be depending on just over £11,000 per year. I want to be living. I want to enjoy my retirement!

There are a few ways you can create and build your own pension pot.

Workplace pension (auto-enrolment)

If you're employed, chances are you've already been auto-enrolled into a workplace pension, and here's how it works:

- You put money in.
- Your employer puts a contribution in too.
- The money is invested until you reach retirement.
- The government adds tax relief.

Every employer must provide a workplace pension scheme, and you'll be automatically enrolled if you're in the UK, over the age of 22 (and below state pension age) and earn more than £10,000 (if you earn less than this, or are younger than 22, you may still be able to opt in, it just won't be automatic).

Your contributions are taken from your monthly salary before it's paid to you, so you don't have to do anything apart from decide how much you want to pay in each month.

Lots of people love to pay into their workplace pension because the more they put in the more their employer contributes. If they match to a certain percentage, this could mean *big free money*.

When I worked for my previous employer, they matched any contributions that I made up to 5% of the value of my monthly pay, so if I paid in £200 a month, they'd also pay in £200 per month! The legal minimum that an employer has to pay is currently 3%, but you'll be able to find out what your employer will match up to by checking your contract or speaking with your HR team.

SIPP (self-invested personal pension)

We'll talk more about these in the next chapter on investing – but a SIPP is a great option if you're self-employed, or you want an extra option to control where your money goes! A SIPP has the option to choose your own investments, so you can choose based on your risk tolerance (whether you want low-, medium- or high-risk investments – you can even choose ethical investment choices).

A pension savings pot

You can simply have a savings pot that is dedicated to your pension as part of your monthly budget, something you save for every month in a high-interest savings account. It doesn't have to be a formal pension account. When I first started thinking about my pension in my early 20s, I set up a standing order of £20 per month to a cash ISA, just to get myself started with saving for my pension, on top of my workplace pension. It doesn't matter how big or small your contributions are when you first start, as long as you start and stay consistent (I'm sorry, I know I always bang on about consistency, but it really is key to so much when it comes to your money).

Planning with a will

I'm telling you straight, you need to have a will in place. It's such a misconception that you only need one if you're rich and wealthy, but here's a few reasons why everybody should have one, regardless of how much money or how many assets you have:

- Without one, your family could be left with stress, legal fees and lots of arguments (trust me, I know from experience that family love to argue over money when it comes to death).
- Your money, however much it is, might not go where you want it to.
- If you've got kids, you need to declare who you want to look after them.
- Even things like your funeral wishes, pets and belongings can be included. It's not just about money.

A will really is practical; if one thing is for certain in life, it's death (sorry, I don't want to get morbid, but we do have a tendency to avoid talking about it when it's one of the surest things we'll all go through).

What to include in a will:

- Who gets what (money, house, car, possessions).
- Guardianship/care wishes for dependents (including your furry kids).
- Where you keep any money, investments, pensions.
- Any funeral wishes.
- You can even opt to have a lasting power of attorney (LPA), who is someone you trust to make decisions if you can't.

My dad passed away when I had just turned 21, and he didn't have a will, and it wasn't the money I cared about, it was the belongings that he had of mine that I never got to see again (messy family issues – let's not go there). A will makes sure that everything is accounted for, leaving your wishes in place, and keeping everything organised. I just think it's such an organised thing to do for your family, and to ensure your last wishes are actually listened to.

If you don't write down your wishes, guess who decides where your things go? The government (mostly) and your family. If you've been organised enough to have your finances in check while you're alive, it's always a sensible idea to carry that one when you pass.

At the time of writing this book, I've had a very close family member in hospital. At one point it was hit and miss (and we are ever so grateful they made it through), but one of the first things on their mind when they woke up after three huge surgeries and being asleep for a week was their will. *True story*. If that's not enough motivation to get one sorted, I don't know what is!

That felt morbid, though I didn't intend to get you worrying about the inevitable, it's not about living in fear of the future, it's just about giving yourself (and your family) options. That's what this whole book has been about, right?

Less of the important morbid stuff, it's time to get into the *rich biz*.

Chapter tasks

- **Action one**: Review your why, make sure you've written it down. Visualise your why.
- **Action two**: Write down your short- and long-term goals, and review them often so you can check in on your progress and adapt where needed.
- **Action three**: Get pension-ready. Get familiar with your workplace pension, if you have one, and if you're self-employed, take a look into SIPP options.
- **Action four**: Get that will written. You'll feel so much better for having it ticked off the life admin to-do list.

CHAPTER 6

INVESTING MADE SIMPLE

DID YOU KNOW that you're an investor already? You may not even realise it but you've been investing for the majority of your life. When you spend in shops, buy a takeaway, go on holiday, you've been investing into somebody else's business, someone else's wealth, helping their money to grow – so why not make your own money grow, and invest for yourself and your family?

Although most of this chapter on investing will be about putting your money to work in the stock market, let's talk about being an investor in all walks of life. Invest in your mindset, your education, your health, your money. You don't need to be a particular type of person to do this.

Investing in yourself

The most important investment you'll ever make… is you.

Whenever we talk investments we automatically think money, or the stock market, but it all starts with investing in you.

If you're not clear on your own money, your goals, or your values, you can't start your stock market investing. Investing in yourself is laying down the foundation first. It's making sure you've taken the time to:

- **Understand your personal finances**: what's coming in, what's going out and where you actually stand.
- **Set your budget**: know how much you can realistically invest.

- **Get clear on your goals**: are you saving for a house? Wanting more freedom? What's the reason you even want to invest?
- **Remember that you owe it to yourself**: too often, we invest into everything but ourselves. We'll spend money on takeaways, nights out, new clothes, and in doing that, it sounds very deep but we're actually investing into someone else's future. Yet we hesitate when it comes to putting money into our own growth.

Why is it that a lot of people wouldn't hesitate to spend £100 on a night out or £50 on shoes, but hesitate to put £20 into themselves? Where does this even come from!

Never forget that you are your biggest asset. When you invest in your mindset, your education, your health and your money, that's when things can really grow.

Yes, we're going to talk about stocks and investing. But before you go putting money into the market, remember that the first investment you need to make is in *you*.

Put your money to work

When I first really thought about investing, I felt overwhelmed before even knowing anything about it. It's normal for someone who grew up where I did to believe that investing is only for the rich, for successful business people and millionaires. Fortunately for us non-millionaires, that mindset is completely wrong. Investing is for *anybody*. Investing is just another way to save your money, it really is as simple as that, but with a chance to make it grow.

I taught myself how to invest because it really is that simple. It sounds so cliché to say that, but it truly is and we have to get rid of those limiting beliefs within ourselves that make us think we aren't capable of investing.

Are we all capable of opening a bank account and saving some money? Yes. Investing is just another way of doing this, but the potential to grow your money is *way* bigger.

The investing we're talking about isn't a get-rich-quick scheme. It's a type of investing that everybody can do and you don't need any advanced knowledge of the stock market or specific complex strategies within finance – but you do need to know a few basics and you have to go into investing with the right mindset knowing it's a long-term thing.

If you're looking for a get rich quick scheme, these usually come with very high risk. The investing we're talking about here is long-term, lower-risk stock market investing (because there's lots of types of investing) such as:

- Bonds (a type of loan you make to a government or big corporation, usually receiving a bit of interest in return).
- Commodities (a fancy word for gold, silver and other physical assets).
- Real estate (houses, properties and all that jazz).

Now of course with investing it's always important to know your money can go up or down. This is not something to get worried about, but you do need to reflect on your appetite for risk before you commit your money to the markets.

So let's dive into the basics!

What are stocks?

So let's imagine you go into your favourite shop, and the guy behind the till says, "We're selling tiny bits of our company. Do you want to buy one?" If you were to say yes and give them some money, you would now own a small part of that company. If the shop does well, gets more customers, makes more money, well then your part goes up in value. They may even share some of the profits with you (these are called 'dividends'). Eventually you decide to sell your part of the company to someone else. By that point, your part is worth more than you paid for it, so you make a tidy profit.

That's exactly how stocks work, but on a bigger scale and on the 'stock market' on an easy-to-use investing app or website rather than someone asking you in-store! When you buy a stock, you're buying a small part of a company like Apple, Tesla or Starbucks. If the company grows and makes more money, your stock becomes more valuable. If things go badly, the stock price can drop.

Now, investing in single stocks (one company) can be a good way to invest your money, but it can be time consuming figuring out what company would be a good one to invest into. We don't like to put all of our eggs into one basket, either, so for people like me who 1) like an easy life and 2) don't like to put all my eggs into one basket, I invest into something called ETFs (exchange-traded funds).

WTF is an ETF?

Let's use chocolate to explain this, because we all love chocolate.

You enter a huge chocolate shop, and you're hungry – for chocolate, of course. But the range is huge and everything looks delicious, so you're not sure which chocolate to go for. So instead of buying one big bar of dairy milk, you buy a box of Celebrations because it's full of different choices! Maltesers, Bounty, Twix, Mars and so on. This means that if one type of chocolate doesn't satisfy your sweet tooth, you still have loads of others to choose from. An ETF offers a similar selection, but instead of chocolate, it contains many relatively small amounts of stock in a large number of companies. And instead of receiving the taste sensation (or unpleasant surprise) of a chocolate, you're receiving the financial gains (or unpleasant surprise) of a company's performance. Because of the diversity of the companies you own, if one company isn't performing too well, it's not too bad because there's lots of others in the same box to make up for it.

This is an investing option that lots of people (like me!) like to use as an easier way to invest. It's typically low risk as it spreads out your risk across lots of different companies (what are the chances all of the companies are doing bad at the same time? Quite low right?). This method of spreading risk across many minor investments is called 'diversification'.

There are ETFs out there that track the 500 largest companies in the USA (S&P 500), including big dogs like Apple, Amazon, Microsoft, and ETFs that track the 250 largest companies in the UK (FTSE 250) like Greggs, Sainsbury's, Pets At Home.

The way I think of it is, imagine having a tiny piece of 500 of the biggest companies in the USA!? Is there ever going to be a day where they all go bust? (If there is, I think we'll have bigger problems on our hands than just worrying about our investments!) If you look at the history of the S&P's growth, you'll see just exactly how well these companies perform and why they're up there being the biggest companies in the world. History and statistics don't lie, and another thing history does is repeats itself. If the history shows us that these companies are growing and growing, why would we not put our money into them?

History doesn't lie

The S&P 500 over the last 20 years has returned (on average) 12.2%. This means that the value of investments made in it increase on average 12.2% per year. Put another way, if you'd invested £100 in an S&P 500 ETF during that time, you could have sold your stock just a year later for £112.20 (on average). That's huge when you think about it, and compare it to the interest rates we get on our bank accounts.

Of course, that doesn't mean every single year was flying high… some years it's up, some years it's down, but when you zoom out and look at the bigger picture, history shows us that the S&P has always gone up over time. That's why so many people (like me, and maybe you now too) invest in ETFs that track it. It's a smaller risk as 1) the history is there to back it up and 2) you're not betting on just one company doing well, you're spreading your money across hundreds.

Historical performance of the S&P 500

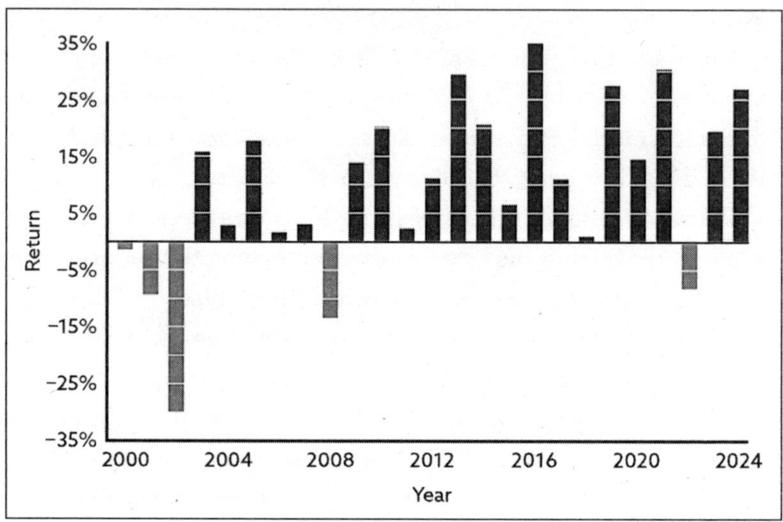

Source: curvo.eu.

Compound interest

Now it's time we start talking about the most important thing ever when it comes to investing…

Compound interest! This is something that every single person needs to understand.

When I truly understood compound interest, it changed my whole outlook on money completely. It really cemented into my brain that our money really can work hard for us, rather than us always working hard for *it*.

Compound interest is a beautiful thing. It basically means you earn interest on interest (then reinvest this interest!), which essentially means that we're going to be rich babyyyyy!

Okay, seriously, it can mean *serious* cash in the bank.

Let's break it down. Imagine you invest £1. Then let's say the interest you earn on that £1 in one year is 10%. This means that one year later you have £1.10. You can take that extra 10p and invest it with the initial £1, so you now have all £1.10 invested.

When the next year comes, you're no longer just earning interest on your £1, you're also earning interest on that additional 10p interest – interest on interest!

So the following year, you then earn 10% interest on your £1.10, which now means you have £1.21. You only invested £1, but now you have 21p extra, just because you're earning interest on interest!

You're probably thinking 'wow really Megan, 21p?' But this is the beauty of compound interest. The bigger the amount, the bigger the reward.

Let's go bigger with the example now. Imagine you have £10,000. You earn 10% interest on this, and after just one year, you now have £11,000. After five years, if you keep reinvesting the interest you earn, you'd have £16,105.10. You've earned £6,105.10

Year 1: £10,000 + 10% = £11,000
Year 2: £11,000 + 10% = £12,100
Year 3: £12,100 + 10% = £13,310
Year 4: £13,310 + 10% = £14,641
Year 5: £14,641 + 10% = £16,105.10

Now imagine you start investing at age 25 for 30 years, and you invest £200 every month, assuming a very modest 7% annual return, by the age of 55, you would have £211,203.76.

Only £72,000 of this would be money that you've put in! The

remaining £139,203.76 comes from the interest earned on your £72,000, thanks to compound interest.

Simple interest versus compound interest

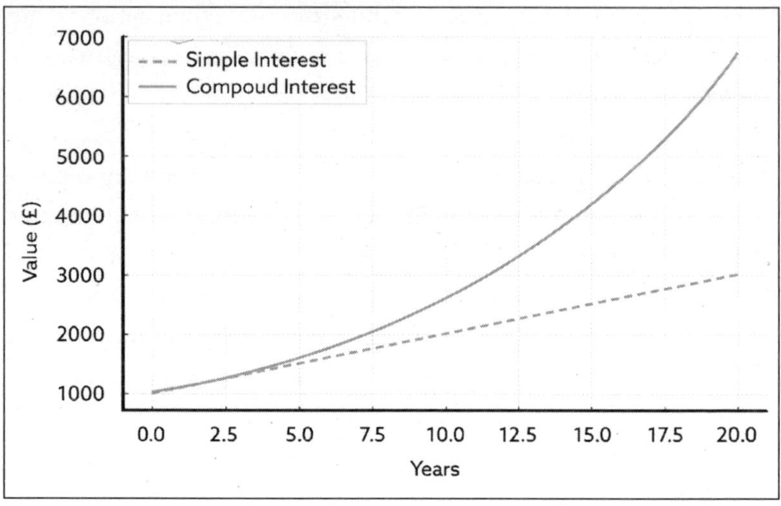

Source: Assumes £1,000 invested with a consistent rate of return of 10% per year over 20 years.

Does that not just blow your mind!? If the answer is no, you need to go and have a play around with a compound interest calculator and see just how crazy the numbers can get. I spend my evenings messing with compound interest calculators; that may sound sad but I find it absolutely fascinating how much money you can grow!

If more people understood this, there'd be way fewer people struggling at retirement age, so I'm really glad you're here reading this book and can get started!

Okay so, some of you may be thinking – Megan! I'm not 25 though! I'm 50! I'm too late!

There's something we talk about when it comes to investing called your 'time horizon'. This is basically the length of time you have to invest your money before needing to access that money. So if you're 50 and plan to retire at 58, you have an eight-year time horizon. The longer the time horizon, the better, however, it's never too late to start investing (how typical does that sound?); this info is also invaluable for you to pass down to your kids!

Yes, you may not have 50 years on your side, but you still have a decent amount of time to start growing your money, and depending on your goals you can start to aggressively invest for impactful returns.

One of my favourite sayings when it comes to investing is 'the best time to start was yesterday, the second-best time to start is now'.

Give your kids five figures for the price of a takeaway

Why is it we all seem to find the money to buy a takeaway, but the majority of us would have to think twice about putting that money into the stock market instead.

The average person in the UK spends £451 per year on takeaway food. If you invested that same money over 18 years, this is how much you could end up with:

The cost of takeaways versus investing

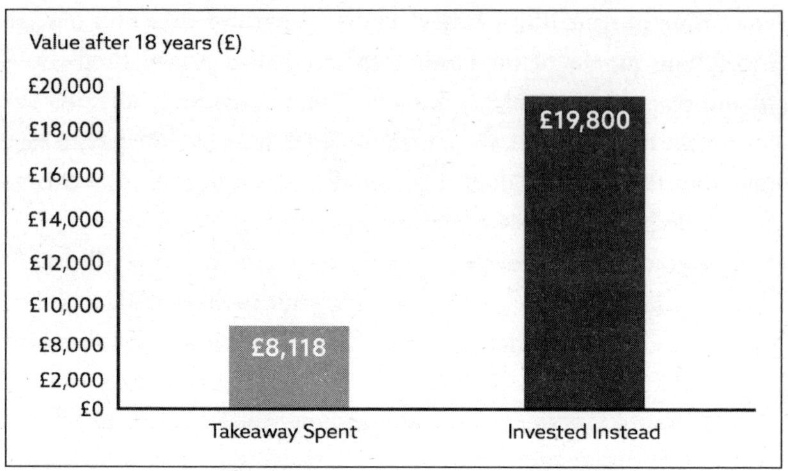

Source: restaurantonline.co.uk. Based on average UK takeaway spend (£8.68 per week) compared with investing the same amount over 18 years at an average rate of return of 6.3% per year.

It's not just you that you can invest for. It's your kids too, and I know their future self will thank you for it. Your kids have a huge time horizon on their hands; they have more time than us, and that's where compound interest will have a huge impact.

The money I invest for my kids could make them a millionaire by retirement age, and that's due to compound interest. Not just my kids though, yours too!

By investing £100 every month until a child turns 18, that will leave them with over £40,000 (assuming a 7% return, which is definitely realistic with the likes of the S&P and its track record!). By the age of 60, even if they don't add another penny to that £40,000-odd (£43,072 to be exact) they'll be millionaires due to that compounding interest. Is it just me or is that wild!? The maths is definitely 'math'ing but I still find it amazing how such a small amount can have such a drastic impact, but that's what you get when you have lots of time on your side, and the gift that keeps on giving which is compound interest.

Please, please do mess around with a compound interest calculator, whether that's to have a look at your own money's potential or for your kids! You'll realise that I'm not actually sad for having this as one of my hobbies. You know people say their guilty pleasure is searching Rightmove for houses they can't afford? Well mine is adding random figures into a compound interest calculator to see how much can really make you a multi-millionaire – and how long it will take for me to afford those Rightmove houses!

So why don't more people invest?

There's lots of reasons why the 'average' person doesn't invest, one being the common myth that we think investing is only for 'rich people' (I used to think that). I didn't come from a family who invested into the stock market, and I didn't learn about it at school, so why would I invest?

The sad truth is that, unlike negativity and secrecy around money, investing is not normalised in society.

Another common reason is that people think investing is too complicated. I took it upon myself to learn about investing, and discovered that it can be an incredibly simple process.

The media will feed you snippets of information about investing that make it feel overwhelming and complicated – things like 'timing the market' 'buy low/sell high' and 'bid/ask spread'.

But don't worry, you won't need any of these to get started.

On top of that, there's:

- **Jargon confusion**: all of the investing language – hearing words like ETFs, dividends, index can sound like another language when you're a newbie.
- **Analysis paralysis**: there are so many different investment choices that people get stuck overthinking and end up doing nothing.

- **Thinking you need loads of money**: some people believe you need thousands to start investing, when in reality you can start with as little as £1!
- **Social media noise**: headlines and content about the market crashing or the next big stock – it can sometimes make it feel like gambling, which can make people hesitate.

The thing is, investing can be complicated, but it depends on your investing style. You can strip it back to basics and keep it simple, just like I do.

I love something called 'dollar-cost averaging' (yes it's still called that in the UK). It's a type of investing method, and completely removes any concern you might have about timing when to buy or when to sell stocks. Basically, all it means is putting a set amount of money into your investments regularly (every month, week, just consistently) no matter what's going on with the market.

Sometimes you'll be buying when the price is high, sometimes when it's low, but over time it averages out. You don't have to stress about timing the market or buying in at the best price. You're just consistently building your pot, and it will smooth itself out as time goes by.

It's such a simple, stress-free way to invest without having to overcomplicate things.

Investing on a budget

You don't have to go big when it comes to investing. You can start with a small amount of money; it's the consistency that's the most important thing. Small amounts over time can add up to a healthy chunk of money, as long as you stay consistent.

As much as I love seeing people change their whole life due to investing, we need to remember that comparing ourselves to others is a trap we want to avoid. Social media can really make you feel like you have to go hard or go home, that if you're not doing something big there's no point doing it at all. But with investing, that simply isn't true.

An investing habit, no matter how small, can do great things for your future. So, would you rather that future-you will be wishing you had started to invest sooner, or glad you started when you did?

Get to grips with the investing basics

When you invest in the stock market, you'll do it through an 'investing platform'. This can be any one of the many reputable websites (or apps) available for this purpose. Find an investing platform that sounds good to you. If you value security, you could choose one of the more recognisable firms – Fidelity or Vanguard, for example. Or if you prioritise user-friendliness, eToro or Trading212 might suit you well. But there are many others available to choose from.

Before committing to any one platform, make sure you compare fees. Investing in a service, and so you will pay the platform provider a small percentage of your investment's value for the privilege (but depending on the platform and the type of investment, it doesn't have to be an amount you will even miss).

You can use comparison sites or your own research to compare the fees of similar investments across different platforms. The lower the fees, the more of your investment returns will go back into your pocket.

Once you've chosen your platform, you'll need to choose the type of account you want to open. This will be your 'tax wrapper', which means it's the account itself (into which you'll put your investments) that will protect your investing earnings from capital gains tax when you come to sell them.

Here's a brief overview of the main types of account you can choose from:

Individual savings accounts (ISAs)

- **Stocks and shares ISA**: if you're 18 or over, you can open a stocks and shares ISA. It's a tax-efficient investment account meaning any money earned inside that account is tax free.
- You can invest up to £20,000 per year (this is the annual ISA allowance) and any growth or dividends (and withdrawals) are tax free. For most investors (and just about all first-time investors) this is the best account to use for your investments.
- **Stocks and shares JISA (junior ISA)**: this is for kids under 18. Parents or guardians can open one, and family/friends can contribute. You can invest up to £9,000 per year.
- This money cannot be withdrawn (but can be transferred to another JISA) and is essentially locked away until your child turns 18. Once they turn 18, the money in this account will automatically become theirs.
- **Lifetime ISA (LISA)**: LISAs can be used to buy your first home or to save for your retirement. You can invest up to £4,000 a year, and the government gives you a 25% bonus (up to £1,000 a year). You need to be aged 18–39 to open one, and you can use it towards a home (up to £450,000) or access it penalty free after 60.
- There are also cash LISAs; you can either have a cash Lisa, stocks and shares LISA or a combination of both. If you do withdraw your money under any circumstances other than buying your first home or reaching retirement, you will be hit with a fee, so make sure this aligns with your goals before opening and investing into one.

Other savings accounts

- **Self-invested personal pension (SIPP)**: a SIPP is a type of pension you can set up yourself. You're able to choose the pension provider and can decide how much you pay in and how often; you can also choose how your money is invested and can choose to manage this yourself. You can have both a SIPP and a workplace pension.

- You will get tax relief on any money you pay into your SIPP and most personal pension providers will claim this automatically for you. This means a £100 contribution will actually cost you £80 as the government will top it up by £20.
- **General investment account (GIA)**: basically the 'current account' of the investing world. It's just a simple, general account. There's no tax-free allowance like with an ISA, so you may pay tax on profits made within the account. There is no limit on how much you can invest, so it's useful if you've maxed your ISA allowance.

Once you've set up an account, you can transfer your money into it and choose the investments you want to buy.

Do not skip this step!

The account itself is not an investment. Too many first-time investors pick a platform, set up their ISA, transfer their money into it and then leave it there.

Tragically, this doesn't get them very far.

This is the point at which you choose from the stocks or funds your platform gives you access to. Most platforms will offer as much information about each product as a professional investor would want to see. This will be much more than you can handle in the early days, so don't worry about reading every Key Information Document for every fund.

By all means look around and compare the options, but as we discussed earlier, for a simple, diversified (low-risk) entry point, you could do worse than to buy an S&P 500 ETF.

Here's a summary of what you need to do before you can get started with investing:

1. Find an investing platform that works for you.
2. Compare platform fees before signing up.
3. Decide on the type of account you want to open (usually a stocks and shares ISA).
4. Choose your investment products (why not start with a simple diversified ETF?).
5. Wait.
6. Profit.

Chapter task

Your checklist to start investing.

- Figure out your time horizon. What are you investing for and how long do you have until you need to access this money?
- How much can you afford to invest every month?
- Find an investment platform to use (make sure you check fees!).
- Decide what investing account you'd like to open.
- Deposit that first amount.

Check these off and you'll be on your way to building wealth!

CHAPTER 7

GET YOUR HUSTLE ON

THE CHAPTER I have been waiting for! If you know me, you know side hustles hold a special place in my heart. They can help us to achieve so much financially, and literally change your life.

I have seen people achieve huge goals, and it was all down to side hustles – things like paying off thousands of pounds worth of debt, buying their first home, booking their first abroad holiday. These are huge milestones that probably wouldn't have been possible without side hustling.

It's not all about the big goals though, even the small things can make a huge difference every month. Having access to an extra £20 to put into your savings, side hustling £50 a month so you can enjoy family takeaways at home. The beautiful thing is, there's no end point when it comes to side hustles; you can earn as little or as much as you like, there's no earning limit and you can use them to achieve anything!

The best bit about side hustles is that *anything* can be a side hustle.

Re-selling clothes. Babysitting. Walking someone's dog. Tutoring. Making candles. Renting out your driveway. There's money in almost everything. And there really is something for everyone – you can find something that works for you.

For me, side hustles changed my life.

- During maternity leave, when SMP didn't even scratch the surface, it was side hustles that kept me financially independent (not having to rely on anybody else has been a big deal to me from a young age).

- When I wanted more time off with my firstborn, side hustle income gave me the freedom to take three more months off unpaid on top of my maternity leave.
- When I was ready to quit my job and go self-employed, side hustles bridged the gap. They gave me confidence because I'd already proven to myself that I could make money outside of my nine-to-five even if my business failed.
- Most months my side hustles actually made me more money than my salary in my corporate job. That was a proper wake-up call, and I realised there is always money to be made.

The Savvy Spender's timeline of side hustles

Let's rewind and test my memory here, because I have done *so* many side hustles over the last decade. You may know some of these already, but others may surprise you.

- **School days**: selling chocolate bars at school. Making personalised masks. Avon rep. Bracelet making.
- **Early adulthood**: forever flower boxes. Event set-up. Sweet boxes. Re-selling.
- **Pre-pandemic and pre-kids**: vegan bakery.
- **Maternity leave**: market research. Surveys. Website testing. Mystery shopping.
- **Mid-to-late 20s (post-children)**: dog walking. Dog sitting. Matched betting.
- **What I still do now**: market research. Website testing. Surveys. Mystery shopping.

Let the side hustles unfold

My side hustle journey started in school, selling the chocolate from my backpack, as you know… but my hustle didn't stop there. I helped my mom with being an Avon rep (remember those days before it all went digital?). I also started creating DIY personalised masks and selling them on eBay; they were popular for hen and stag parties and the faces we were sent were always entertaining!

After leaving school, while working my part-time jobs, I launched a 'forever flower' small business. I made floral arrangements that would last forever for occasions like Valentine's Day. I used to spend my evenings and weekends going to the wholesalers and buying my stock. I felt like I lived there, constantly visiting because I'd never have enough money to buy my stock in bulk! This little business evolved into another business when customers began asking to hire my flower boxes for events, which led me to start an events business called Pretty Additions. I invested in a sweet cart, doughnut stands, lots of cute decorations, and I charged to set up for baby showers, parties and weddings.

While all this was going on, I'd see my mum coming home from in-person market research studies with cash in an envelope. I obviously had to be involved and asked her to introduce me to her contact… and that was the start of a new chain of side hustles!

As the events business got busier, I actually struggled to keep up as a one-man band. I was transporting all the equipment to events by myself, in my little car, every weekend, and it became overwhelming and exhausting. I decided to sell the business for a small profit and moved on to my next venture: a vegan bakery. This was honestly amazing; we rented out a nearby kitchen and sold our cakes from there. We also hosted afternoon teas as the kitchen has an indoor dining space. We loved it (I set it up with my sister-in-law), but unfortunately, the pandemic hit and caused lots of businesses to close (just like us), and it timed perfectly. This was when I found out I was pregnant with my firstborn: perfect timing!

During the pandemic, and pregnancy, my digital side hustles ramped up! Things like website testing, market research, surveys and much more became my babies. While on maternity leave, I ended up making over £10,000 from my side hustles!

This journey wasn't just about making extra money (although that bit was obviously great; it taught me so much more about the money world all around us.

So why am I telling you my side hustle life story? Well it's because I want you to really understand why they hold such a place in my heart, and what they can actually do to change your life, just like they did mine.

I really want to hit home that anything can be a side hustle. It's never been easier to make money in this digital age. We have access to millions of people at the click of a button, not only to sell to, or to make money from, but to get inspiration from.

Let your imagination run wild

I've been side hustling for over a decade and it still blows my mind at how many ways there are to make money. Let's give you some weird and wonderful ways so you can really feel what I'm trying to say!

- Renting out their driveway for commuters (a family member that lives close to an airport does this and makes passive money from it every month!).
- Walking dogs or even just sitting with cats while owners are away (I've done these and loved every minute!).

- Reselling items from charity shops on eBay or Vinted (I know re-sellers personally who have made a successful business out of re-selling).
- Voiceover work for brands and UGC (user-generated content).
- Testing apps and websites.
- Renting out a spare room on Airbnb.
- Mystery shopping and getting paid to eat out.
- Online tutoring, using your specialities.

They're all a tad random, and maybe quite niche – but that's the beauty of side hustles, there really is something for everyone.

Do what you enjoy

As you know by now, it's never *just* about the money, and when choosing a side hustle it's important to choose something you love if you want to keep it consistent.

So, let's think about what you love, what do you enjoy, what are you good at, what skills do you have?

Think about these:

- Do you have a skill you can teach (tutoring, coaching, lessons, digital courses)?
- Do you enjoy physical work, being on the move (dog walking, cleaning, gardening)?
- Do you prefer flexible, online work (freelancing, surveys, blogging)?
- Do you want quick cash or something slower but more consistent?

Time is of course a huge factor when it comes to side hustling.

When you're looking after tiny humans or have a physically demanding job, you may not have the time or the mental capacity to pick up a huge demanding side hustle – and I'm not here to advocate burning out for money… and that is why I love side hustles (how many times will I actually say this during this chapter?); you can choose how little or how much time you want to spend on a side hustle depending on your lifestyle and goals!

If you're a stay-at-home mum you might find doing market research or surveys fit around your little one's nap times. If you're someone who loves being out and about or shopping you could take up mystery shopping, or re-selling. Someone who is time poor and needs something as passive as it can be, renting out your driveway or selling digital products could be more up your street.

These are just examples, but it shows the vast range of side hustles out there that can suit different lifestyles.

A side hustle can be just that, something you pick up and drop off on the side whenever you feel you need a little extra money, or when you're working towards a particular goal, or it can be something more consistent that brings you in a similar amount every month and could even become a full-time business. The freedom is yours to do as you wish with a side hustle.

Some hustles need zero upfront investment. If you have a phone and Wi-Fi, you can start almost instantly to make some money. Think about online surveys, matched betting or mystery shopping. These won't make you a millionaire, but they can add up to hundreds of pounds a month, and sometimes that's the difference between dipping into your overdraft or being able to add to your savings pot.

Then there are hustles that use what you already know. Maybe you're a maths genius and could tutor online. Maybe you've got a car and could deliver food in the evenings. Maybe you're the organised pal who could start managing other people's diaries as a virtual assistant. These don't require any new qualifications, just skills and attributes you already have, so use them!

And then, there are the more structured, qualification-based side hustles. These take time (and sometimes money) to set up, but they often come with higher earning potential and even the potential to be turned into a full-time business.

- A qualified accountant could take on a few bookkeeping clients.
- If you love animals, dog grooming demand is growing, and a small course can get you started.
- Beauty-based skills like nail tech, lash tech or hair extensions can bring in hundreds of pounds a week, especially if you build on socials and get a good client base!

Avoid hustle culture burnout

A 2023 study from Henley Business School found that 25% of UK adults now have a side hustle.[15] Those side hustles aren't generating small amounts, either! One in ten hustlers report making over £5,000 in additional income.

Another report showed that side hustles boomed after the pandemic (unsurprisingly), with over a quarter of hustlers saying their side hustle income was essential just to keep up with the cost of living.[16]

But despite being on the rise, hustle culture gets a bad rep online. You've probably seen the posts that basically glamourise working 16-hour days, never saying no, never resting and basically promoting burnout… hate to point out the obvious but that's not healthy…

What I will say though, is there's a balance. Working hard for your goals is not toxic. Somewhere along the line, like a lot of things, social media twisted the meaning of 'hustle' and the output leads people to thinking it's a toxic thing to do.

Hustling doesn't have to mean grinding yourself into the ground. It's about being intentional with your time and energy. If you do want more out of life, and need more money to do that, whether that's reaching financial freedom, more holidays or paying off debt, you may have to put in some extra work to get there.

There's also a big difference between working hard and working smart. If you're time poor (like me), you don't need to chase every £10 gig you find. Some things really aren't worth the money. You need to find the high-paying hustles that really pay well for your time. For example, I never apply for a market research study unless it's at least £60 per hour. Anything less isn't worth the sacrifice for me.

Of course resting is important, yes, but so is putting in the effort to change your life. Balance is key. You don't need to work every hour of every day, but you do need to be prepared to work harder than 'normal' if you want results that aren't 'normal'.

It's a sad reality that for many, a side hustle is essential for survival, not a nice luxurious extra. The silver lining though is that they're so easily accessible. They also help relieve the pressure we feel when we only have one income.

If you're not sure where to start on your side hustle journey, here's three of my favourite side hustles that anybody can do if they wanted to. They're accessible, don't cost anything to do, don't require any skill and can make you a decent chunk of money.

1. Market research

You literally get paid to speak your opinion. Market research is hands down one of my favourite side hustles! It's also one of the easiest for almost anyone to get started with, and arguably one of the ones with a great hourly rate of pay.

How does it work?

Companies want to know what the general public thinks before they launch something new. That could be anything from a chocolate bar, to a perfume ad, to a banking app. They're looking for honest, everyday feedback and they'll pay you for it.

Why do companies pay for this?

Because if they launch something without testing it, they could lose millions. Imagine creating a fancy new website that customers find confusing, or designing packaging that people actually dislike. That's where we come in. Our feedback helps brands avoid mistakes and gives them the invaluable opinions of the people they are selling to, and then they reward us for our time and opinion.

Over the years I've done all sorts of market research studies. I've watched perfume adverts that never even made it to TV. I've been asked to give feedback on chocolate packaging and even had to draw my own. I've had conversations about my bank, why I chose them, what keeps me with them, what frustrates me about their service. There are all different types of ways these conversations take place. It can either be a one-to-one phone call, a group call, an online community chat type thing, or sometimes even in person. (Most market research studies were in person pre-pandemic but of course most things went digital post the pandemic – which is a win for the side hustle community as it makes it easier to make money from the comfort of your own home.)

My highest-paying study was £300 for a home visit where two researchers came to my house to discuss my eating habits. To this day, I don't actually know what brand or product it was for; sometimes they never tell you. But that's part of the fun. You go in for the money, and come away having enjoyed the process (or maybe I'm just easily pleased!).

It's flexible, it's varied and it's often really enjoyable. You're not just filling in endless surveys (though those exist too), you're part of shaping what companies put out into the world. It's one of those hustles that proves you don't need special skills, qualifications or hours of free time. You just need your opinion, and we all have one of those!

An easy way to find sites to use to apply for these types of studies is to simply Google 'market research websites'; however, at the time of writing this, there are two sites that I would really recommend to help you get started:

- **Respondent.io**: worldwide and you can easily apply via their website; they have opportunities that pop up every day.
- **Dscout**: this is an app that you can download on your phone's app store. Always lots of opportunities to apply for and lots about finance too, which always suits me!

2. Mystery shopping

I'll be honest, I didn't even think mystery shopping was a real thing until I started doing it myself. I thought it was one of those internet myths but it really is legitimate, and it's another one of my favourite side hustles.

I always recommend this one to mums, especially while on maternity leave as it can get you out the house which, is always needed with a new baby, but you're also earning money at the same time!

So how does it work?

Companies ask for mystery shoppers to check up on their customer service, product quality and overall experience. Instead of just trusting what managers or staff say, they send in real customers (like you and me) to report back on how things *actually* are. It could be anything from how quickly you're greeted at a fast-food counter, to whether a shop assistant recommends the right product or up-sells as they're supposed to, or even how clean a restaurant looks. Your job is basically to go in, try out the service and then give honest feedback afterwards.

This is great for people who love experiences, eating out, going bowling, testing new products. You usually get your meal, day out or item covered and you get paid for it, so it's a proper win-win. It's not the biggest earner in the world, but when you think about it, you're getting freebies that you'd probably spend money on anyway. If you're savvy with it, it can free up money in your budget for other things.

I've had some brilliant freebies from mystery shopping. I've eaten free pizza; I've been sent to try out burgers. I've even been paid to go bowling. One of the strangest but funniest tasks I've done was phoning a fast-food pizza shop to test their customer service, basically playing the role of an annoying customer with questions then reporting back on how they handled it.

It might not make you thousands, but it's a great example of how side hustles don't always have to be about big money. Sometimes it's about the value you get back in experiences. Things you'd usually happily pay for, but instead you get them for free (and often with some cash on top).

Mystery shopping sites and companies can vary depending on location, so to find them it's best to search online. But take a look and you'll find that this really is a worldwide side hustle!

3. Surveys

Don't come at me for this one. I know surveys get a bad rep. You either love them or you hate them. People say they're 'pennies for your time'... but like I always say, only do what's worth your time, and that'll be different for everybody.

The reason I love them and recommend them for beginners... You can pick them up at *any* time of day. They're made for those little 'dead time' moments. Waiting for the kettle to boil, waiting for the kids to finish school, sitting through the night feeds when you're trying to keep your eyes open, waiting for the adverts to finish on the TV. Instead of aimlessly scrolling TikTok or Instagram, you could be finishing a survey and earning a few pence or a few pounds. Trust me, it really adds up over time. Remember: look after the pennies and the pounds take care of themselves.

Another thing people don't realise is that small surveys can sometimes open the door to bigger market research opportunities. You might start with a 50p survey, but then get invited into a focus group paying £50 for an hour of your time.

I even got my mum into surveys. Now she absolutely loves them. She's set herself a side hustle goal of making £50 a month from surveys, which she then cashes out as an Asda voucher to help with her food shop. It's not lifechanging money, but it makes an actual difference to her budget every month and frees up cash that she can do other things with.

They're low effort, flexible and you can literally do them in your pyjamas at midnight if you want to.

Let me reiterate: surveys aren't going to replace your full-time job, but as a little trickle of extra income, they can be worth doing to dip your toe into side hustles. And if you're going to be glued to your phone anyway, why not make some money from it!

Survey sites and apps change so rapidly – they close down, a new one pops up, so it's best to stay up to date with the best survey apps to use by following along on social media and getting involved with the side hustle community!

The bonus one: website testing

You really thought I could stop at my top three? I had to throw in another! I've got a soft spot for website testing because it was one of the side hustles that played a big part in earning extra money while I was on maternity leave. I was able to log onto my laptop when my baby was asleep and earn some extra money almost instantly.

In simple terms, companies pay everyday people like you and me to test out their websites, apps or even prototypes before they go live. Businesses want to know: is the website easy to use? Can customers find what they're looking for? Do the buttons make sense? Does the checkout process feel smooth, or is it confusing? They don't just want an expert's opinion, they want real feedback from real users, because that's who will be using their site when it's launched.

So how does it work? You sign up with a testing platform (my personal favourite has always been UserTesting). They'll send you instructions to do a task, something like 'look for a jumper on this website and try to add it to your basket', and as you go through the process, you speak your thoughts out loud so the company can literally hear your frustrations, anything you find confusing or easy. Sometimes it's as quick as five or ten minutes, and you get paid for each test you complete.

I just love how accessible this side hustle is. It's like market research but easier, because you get chosen instantly and you can complete tasks at any time of day or night.

Website testing on UserTesting is open to multiple countries. So whether you're in the UK, US or even somewhere else, this site will be available for you, but there are many others out there too.

Pay your dues

People often ask me whether they need to pay income tax on their side hustles more times than you could imagine, and, hey, I'm glad people are asking, but if there's one thing for sure in this life, it's taxes (especially in the UK!). If you're earning extra money, the chances you have to pay tax on it is high.

There are some side hustles that are actually tax free, but most, unfortunately, aren't.

In the UK there's something called the trading allowance. If you're in the UK, you can earn up to £1,000 in side-gig/casual/self-employment income per tax year without paying tax or needing to report it. If you earn more than £1,000, you'll need to declare the extra, or deduct expenses if that gives you a better deal. This is correct as at 2025, but it's always worth checking the government website to stay up to date with any changes (and if you're not in the UK, check with an accountant).

Now, I'm not a tax advisor, and I highly recommend you speak with an accountant or financial advisor when it comes to your taxes and side hustles, but please, please do not let tax put you off making more money!

Don't put yourself in a box!

This is where confidence with money comes creeping back in. So many people put themselves in a box when it comes to their earning potential because they're scared of the dreaded *tax*. I can't tell you how many times I've heard things like "I don't want to take on more work, I'll get taxed more", or "There's no point in a side hustle if it all goes to the taxman."

That mindset is holding you back. Yes, you'll pay tax if you earn more. That's how the system works. But you are still earning more! *You will always take home more than if you didn't earn it at all.* If you earn an extra £500 and pay 20% tax, you still walk away with £400. If you didn't do it because you didn't want to 'get taxed' you'd walk away with... 0.

I don't know about you, but I'd rather have £400 extra in my pocket than nothing at all. Trust me, tax isn't worth not pushing yourself to earn more money!

The fear of crossing into a higher tax bracket is another one that stops people. Here's the truth that usually gets people confused: when you move into a new tax bracket, only the money *above the threshold* is taxed at the higher rate, not everything you earn. So if you move from the 20% to 40% tax bracket, it doesn't suddenly mean you're handing over almost half your income. You're just paying a higher rate on the bit above that threshold.

So please, don't cap your own earning potential because you're worried about paying some extra tax. The government will always take their share, but you'll always keep yours too.

Choose wisely

With the rise of hustle culture, unavoidably there's also been a rise in scams. With the economic crisis leaving a lot of people in a position of struggle, this is where scammers will try their luck. They know people are feeling vulnerable when it comes to money and will try anything to make some extra money.

When it comes to side hustles, I don't really like the term 'if it's too good to be true, it probably is' because if I told someone I got paid £60 to eat a burger, they'd probably think that sounds too good to be true! But still, it's a good little reminder to keep at the back of your mind. If something feels off, pause and check it out before you hand over your time or money.

A few red flags to watch out for:

- **Upfront fees**: you should never have to pay to join or do a side hustle. None of the sites I've used for side hustles have ever charged me an upfront fee. Real opportunities pay you, not the other way around.
- **Multi-level marketing schemes (MLMs)**: these are often dressed up as 'business opportunities' where you join a team and then make money by recruiting others. While some people make money in MLMs, the stats show most don't, and many actually lose money.
- **Unrealistic promises**: 'earn £5,000 a week working two hours from your phone!' Just no. That's not how genuine hustles work. This is definitely too good to be true (and now my £60 burger tasting sounds way more realistic).
- **Vague job descriptions**: if you can't get a straight answer about what you'll actually be doing, that's usually a sign that it's not as clear cut as it seems.

And a quick note on the digital marketing/course-selling world: not everything out there is a scam, there are genuine courses that teach valuable skills and can lead to real income. But not everyone selling them is being fully transparent.

The rule of thumb: if someone is promising easy money with zero effort, or the only thing they seem to be making money from is teaching *others* how to make money, take it with a big pinch of salt.

Protecting yourself is about using common sense, doing your research and not letting the excitement of quick cash cloud your judgement. A real side hustle might not make you rich overnight, but it will provide you with consistent income that is real and can work for anybody.

Balancing life and hustles

Side hustles are meant to be an addition to your life, not completely take over all of the spare time you have. The biggest mistake I see (and honestly, I was guilty of this myself when I first started) is letting your hustle take over every spare moment you have because of how tempting it is to just pick it up whenever you can… but believe me, it'll burn you out.

The beauty of a side hustle is that you get to decide how much time you put into it. Some weeks you might feel like going all in, and other weeks life will get in the way.

Progress is still progress, even if it's slow. The trick is always *consistency* and making sure it fits into your lifestyle in a healthy way.

Here's a few tips that have really helped me juggle side hustles alongside real life:

- **Set boundaries**: if you say you're only going to side hustle for three hours a week, stick to it. Don't let it eat into your family time or your rest.

- **Time block**: instead of trying to do little bits every single day, especially in the beginning, dedicate one block of time (like a Saturday morning nap time or a couple of evenings a week) so you can focus and not feel overwhelmed.
- **Start with one**: it's easy to be like a kid in a sweetshop when you first delve into the world of side hustles, but that way can get overwhelming quickly. Start with one you like the sound of. Once you've found your feet with that one, then try adding another in.
- **Know your worth**: if you're short on time, don't waste it on low-paying tasks. It's okay to be picky. I used to get caught up on working for pittance just because I thought extra money is still money, but I quickly realised that you have to know your worth.
- **Use 'dead time'**: Waiting for the kettle to boil? On a night feed? Sat in the car waiting for the kids? Catch yourself aimlessly scrolling? Those pockets of time are perfect for quick wins like surveys or applying for market research.

At the end of the day, your side hustle is there to work *for you*. It's a tool to give you more money, but it shouldn't take all of your spare time away. As long as you keep your goals in mind, you'll find the balance that works for your life.

Chapter tasks

Action: Think about what you enjoy, how much time you have to spare and how much extra money you'd realistically like to earn per month. Then you can choose a side hustle that will suit you.

CONCLUSION: YOUR FINANCIAL FUTURE

When you first picked up this book, you may have felt a mixture of excitement, curiosity and maybe even a little bit of dread (I hope not, but it is normal!). Money has the ability to mix up so many emotions in us, and many we've spoken about… fear, shame, guilt, hope, excitement. All of these play a part in how we think about money.

I hope this book has taught you that, wherever you are with your money journey right now, you're in the driving seat. Even if it might not feel that way just yet. Maybe you're in debt and it feels never-ending. Maybe your spending habits are a little impulsive. Maybe you've never budgeted in your life and the thought of it makes you want to throw this book out of the window (please don't). Wherever you are, it's easy to feel like money controls you instead of the other way around.

But guess what!? Now, you are absolutely loaded with the tools. You've worked through (or are about to work through) the action points in these chapters. You've learned about mindset, how to shift to a positive money mindset, how to unlearn those habits we picked up at a young age, and how shifting from scarcity to abundance can change everything. You've learned practical steps like budgeting, building an emergency fund, mindful spending, setting up your bank accounts, and even investing and side hustling. You've seen how small tweaks in your habits can lead to huge shifts over time.

You're now in the position to create your financial future, and not just let it be something that plays out without your input.

Your financial future really is in your hands.

Now to implement

Reading this book was step one. It's a huge step even to acknowledge you need to learn more about money, but knowledge without action is just expensive entertainment. Don't do yourself the disservice of paying for this book, and then not taking the action!

The money magic happens when you implement what you've actually learned.

So, if you haven't already, I want you to go back through the action points at the end of each chapter and start working through them. I'm not going to tell you off for not doing them, but I want you to get your money's worth from this book to actually change your future, and I'm sure you want that too!

Here's a little tick list to help you get started:

- **Shift your mindset**: think about your money habits, your money mindset, what has influenced you up until now and what steps you can put into place to start to reframe your thinking.
- **Think about your spending triggers**: and how you can put blockers in place to avoid impulse spending and become more mindful.
- **Know your why**: make sure you're clear on your 'why'. This will be your motivation and driving force, especially in the early days of starting your money journey.

- **Build your budget**: pick a budgeting method and trial it; create that plan (remember, you want to tell your money where to go, instead of wondering where it went).
- **Start your emergency fund**: it doesn't matter if you start small, just get it started, you can always up it at a later date.
- **Try a spending challenge**: to see if it works for you (no-spend days, low-spend weekends).
- **Separate your bank accounts**: bills in one, spending in another. You can start to look into extra savings pots for those sinking funds.
- **Look into side hustles**: have a think about what you're good at, what you enjoy and how much time you have spare to dedicate to it.
- **Schedule money dates**: you could even set up some with your partner. Get them in your calendar now so they're already planned.
- **Set goals**: short term and long term, so you know what you're working towards.
- **Start to plan for the future**: think about investing for yourself, your kids, your retirement.
- **Start to talk about money**: you're making this your lifestyle, so now you can add to the mission to make money less of a taboo subject. Talk out loud and be confident about money, and get the people around you talking too!

These are your first building blocks, along with the action points in each chapter. I'm going full-blown teacher on you but work through them at your own pace, there's no deadline. There's not even a finish line, because this is a journey – and it's an ever-evolving one.

Allow me to encourage you

Throughout this book, I've shared tips, advice and strategies. I talk about money all day every day, and you might be thinking *it's easy for you to say all this, you've figured it all out.*

If you are thinking that, I'll tell you now: I don't have it all figured out. I'm still on my money journey, just like you. I'm still learning, still making mistakes, still navigating new challenges as life changes.

I didn't wake up one day magically good with money. I learned through years of trial and error. I've made financial mistakes, some small, some big (they were all lessons learned). I've had to unlearn old habits. I've spent thousands on my own financial education, reading, listening, adapting.

You're going to have bumps in the road, and you're going to feel like you're behind (you're not!); it's going to feel hard sometimes. Some of it will feel hard. If you fall off track, don't beat yourself up, just pick yourself up and keep going. Progress is not about being perfect, because quite frankly perfect is a myth! But it is about being consistent.

Talk money

Too many of us were raised to believe that talking about money is rude, awkward or shameful. But keeping quiet is what keeps people stuck. If nobody talks about money, how do we learn? How do we grow? How do we break out of old patterns and bad advice passed down through generations?

So, I'm asking you to be part of the change. Start talking about money. With your friends, your partner, your kids, your family. The more we talk, the less alone people feel. The more we share, the more opportunities people can see for themselves. And the more normal it becomes!

Money doesn't have to be taboo. It can be a tool we learn about, share tips about, help each other to grow and even help each other make more of it!

Invest in yourself

Always remember that you are your biggest investment.

Your earning potential, your knowledge, your confidence – you are learning to take control of these, and they are all part of your assets.

Investing in yourself doesn't always mean spending money. It can be as simple as setting aside 20 minutes to read about money every week, listening to a podcast, taking an online course. Most importantly, it's simply saying yes to opportunities to help you to grow and learn.

Every book you read, every conversation you have, every skill you learn compounds over time. Just like money, knowledge grows with consistency.

So make it your mission to never stop learning.

Be kind to yourself

This is a journey, and is there ever a journey that's smooth from start to finish? You're going to make mistakes, mess up, get things wrong – but that is okay!

The worst thing you can do is let these things ruin your whole journey. Remember that mistakes aren't failures, they're lessons learned.

So, be kind to yourself. Celebrate the wins, no matter how small. A £10 saving is just as worthy of celebration as a £1,000 one, because both mean you're moving in the right direction. Don't downplay your progress just because it feels small. Small steps, consistently, are what lead to massive change.

Keep your goals in mind

At the end of the day, money isn't really about money. It's about what money allows you to do, and what you want it to do for you. It's the freedom. The security. The choices it brings.

So, always keep your goals and your *why* at the forefront of your mind and never lose sight of them. When you're tempted to overspend, when budgeting feels boring, when saving feels hard, remember what you're working towards. Your *why* is what will always keep you going.

The future is yours

It's been an emotional one, and it's time to continue your journey. But where do you go from here? Well, you simply keep going. You keep learning, adjusting, implementing, celebrating and trying!

Your financial journey will not look like anyone else's, because this is your life, your money and your future. Don't compare it to anyone else's.

You now have the tools, the mindset and the power to create the financial future you want.

You're not stuck in the patterns of previous generations. You're in control.

When you get there, exactly where you want to be (and you will get there), you'll look back and realise that every small change, every little shift in mindset, every consistent habit added up to that very moment.

ENDNOTES

1 Mark my words I'll win another award soon enough! (Maybe I even have since writing this – you'll have to Google me and find out.)

2 www.barclays.co.uk/smart-investor/news-and-research/gender-gap-in-investments

3 maps.org.uk/en/media-centre/press-releases/2021/24-million-uk-adults-dont-feel-confident-managing-their-money-talk-money-week-is-here-to-help

4 www.virginmoneyukplc.com/newsroom/article/brits-reveal-they-feel-comfortable-talking-to-friends-about-money

5 hbr.org/2020/11/what-you-should-follow-instead-of-your-passion

6 For readers outside of the UK, B&M is a shop that sells *everything* (but it's not as good as Target in the US). Bedding, chocolate, pet supplies, books, garden furniture. Anything you need, you can find it in B&M.

7 www.independent.co.uk/life-style/food-shopping-unhealthy-hungry-supermarkets-survey-results-a9143026

8 commonslibrary.parliament.uk/research-briefings/cbp-7584

9 metopayfinance.com/does-everyone-have-debt-uk

10 metopayfinance.com/does-everyone-have-debt-uk

11 www.upskillist.com/blog/why-celebrating-small-wins-boosts-motivation/#:~:text=According%20to%20research%20by%20Teresa,Boosting%20Confidence%20and%20Self%2DEfficacy

12 www.starlingbank.com/news/money-matters-top-cause-of-arguments-among-couples

13 www.virginmoneyukplc.com/newsroom/article/money-worries-sleepless-nights

14 andysmanclub.co.uk/understanding-debt-mental-health-with-stepchange

15 www.simplybusiness.co.uk/about-us/press-releases/side-hustles

16 www.ipse.co.uk/campaigns/other-campaigns/making-the-case-for-freelancers-report

ACKNOWLEDGEMENTS

THE BIGGEST THANKS goes to my partner, who not only encouraged my financial journey but inspired me to go for a book deal, and helped me to find the right words every now and again during the writing stage for this book.

And the next most important thanks goes to you, the reader. Thank you for allowing me to help you with whatever stage you're at on your money journey. It's a privilege to be part of your journey.

ABOUT THE AUTHOR

MEGAN MICKLEWRIGHT was passionate about money from a young age, always looking for ways to make, save and grow what she had. During maternity leave with her firstborn she began sharing her journey online, opening up about money and the financial lessons she'd learnt along the way. This grew into a savvy community of thousands who have connected with this real approach to money.

Now a mum of two, Megan helps families feel more in control of their money by sharing ways to make, save and grow more of it. As a content creator, presenter, educator and author of *The Savvy Spender*, she's become a trusted voice in the personal finance space, showing that small habits and consistent steps really can change your life.